A *doorway* into magic . . .

Justin noticed an odd mist creeping around the base of the tree—a mist that seemed somehow to have more light, more color, than it should. As he circled the tree, he heard a whispering sound and felt a tingle in his skin. The mist covered the street ahead of him—a street he had never seen before, despite the fact that Barker's Elbow was a very small town.

He walked on. At the end of the street he saw a strange, old-fashioned building. In the window were the words

ELIVES MAGIC SUPPLIES
S. H. ELIVES, PROP.

I sure could use a little magic about now, thought Justin. He glanced at his watch. Most of the stores in town were closed by this time of the evening. But this one had a light in the window.

He tried the door. It opened smoothly.

A small bell tinkled overhead as he stepped inside. . . .

Look for the complete set of Bruce Coville's anthologies of scary stories:

BRUCE COVILLE'S
BOOK OF

MAGIC II
MORE TALES TO CAST A SPELL ON YOU

Compiled and edited by
Bruce Coville

Assisted by
Lisa Meltzer

Illustrated by
John Pierard

A GLC Book

AN
APPLE
PAPERBACK

SCHOLASTIC INC.
New York Toronto London Auckland Sydney

For John Pierard,
**who has brought talent, imagination, and great weirdness
to these books.**

ISBN 0-590-85297-3

12 11 10 9 8 7 6 5 4 3 2 1   7 8 9/9 0 2/0

Printed in the U.S.A.   40

First Scholastic printing, July 1997

CONTENTS

Contents

INTRODUCTION:

Mr. Cranky Says Goodbye

Well, here it is, gang. The end of the road, the last book in the set, the final volume that brings us to an even dozen *Bruce Coville's Books of All Sorts of Weird Things*.

I hope you've enjoyed them. (From the mail I get, I'd say you have.) They've been a lot of hard work for our team, but I'm pretty proud of what we've accomplished.

One of the things I'm most pleased about is that we have provided a home for *long* short stories.

See, there's something weird about children's magazines in this country: they all insist on fairly short stories—as if kids have limited attention spans or are too dumb to read something longer. So during the four years that we have been working on this series, these books have been one of the very few places that someone who writes for kids could tell a short story that was more than two thousand words long.

Which means that these books were about the only place a reader like you could find such stories—stories where the writers had the pages necessary to tell a longer, more complex story than they could do in eight pages. (Which is not to say that we let our writers sprawl all over the place. We always tried to tighten the stories, making the writing sharper and more focused.)

In one way, an insistence on short, simple stories in most places is no surprise. This country has a lot of weird ideas about kids and how to treat them. The people who make cereal and toys look at you not as people, but customers. ("Get those kids to buy! Buy! BUY!") Schools, too often, look at you as their product. ("We are going to produce good citizens who will go out and work hard and buy! Buy! BUY!") And publishers, who really ought to know better, too often look at you as dopes who aren't willing to read long books with big words. ("Kids won't get it!")

(Heh. If they think kids don't get it, they ought to take a look at what adults don't get.)

Well, I do sound grouchy today, don't I? But, you know, I've devoted the last twenty-five years of my life to working for and with kids, and I get cranky when I see people not taking them seriously, not giving them credit for what they can do, how deeply they think and feel.

What's all this got to do with magic?

Well, magic is just one form of power—a way to make things happen. And your whole job as a kid is to *get* power. You start out with none (we're all born naked, ugly, and helpless) and gather it as you go along.

Your power comes from what you learn. Every skill you pick up, every bit of knowledge you add to the pile, gives you more power in the world. When you want a cookie and all you can do is scream, you have very limited power.

When you learn to say, "Mother, please give me a cookie, or I'll bite you," you have more power.

And when you learn to make cookies yourself, you have real power.

Now the truth is, the way you get power is by hard work.

"Jeez," I can hear you say. "Where's the magic in *that?*"

Depends, I suppose, on how you define magic.

One major aspect of magic, as you'll find in the stories that follow, is *transformation*—the changing of one thing into another. Fast transformations are more spectacular—but often less likely to last. Transformations that take time, like the transformation of an infant to an adult, the slow addition of bone and muscle and brain and skill, is something solid and real and a miracle beyond anything our science can now create.

A sort of magic, if you will.

And that's what you're about as a kid. You're gathering your power, preparing yourself to enter the world and transform it with the magic of your strength and your knowledge and your righteous anger at all that is wrong that doesn't need to be.

Of course, there are plenty of reasons to have some fun along the way!

Which is why we've put together this book for you. In the pages that follow you'll find wizards and unicorns, magic shops and dragons, weird spells and wacky fairy godmothers. Everything, in short, that I look for myself when I read a book of magic.

And if the stories are longer and stronger and stranger than you find in most other places—well, don't tell the grown-ups.

What they don't know won't hurt them.

Bruce Coville

Mr. Elives' Magic Shop is one of my favorite places to visit. Usually when I write about the shop, it is in the form of a novel, such as Jeremy Thatcher, Dragon Hatcher *or* Jennifer Murdley's Toad. *Here's a shorter story, about what happens when a boy named Justin Jones stumbles into the shop in need of a way to change his life.*

I originally wrote this story to perform with the Syracuse Symphony. But every time we do the piece, I get numerous requests from people who want to know where they can find the story in print form. So here it is.

THE METAMORPHOSIS OF JUSTIN JONES

Bruce Coville

Justin Jones shot out the front door of the house where he lived—not *his* house, just the place where he was forced to live—and ran until he could no longer hear his uncle's

1

shouts. Even then he didn't feel safe. Sometimes Uncle Rafe's anger was so powerful it propelled the man onto the street after Justin. So the boy ran on, stopping only when the stitch in his side became so painful he could go no farther.

He leaned against a tree, panting and gasping for breath. The air burned in his lungs.

It was late twilight, and stars had just begun to appear, peeking out of the darkness like the eyes of cats hiding in a closet. Justin didn't see them. He was pressing his face against the tree, wishing he could melt into its rough bark and be safe.

When he finally opened his eyes again, Justin noticed an odd mist creeping around the base of the tree—a mist that seemed somehow to have more light, more color, than it should.

Curious, he stepped forward to investigate.

As he circled the tree, he heard a whispering sound and felt a tingle in his skin. The mist covered the street ahead of him—a street he had never seen before, despite the fact that Barker's Elbow was a very small town.

He walked on.

At the end of the street he saw a strange, old-fashioned-looking building. In the window were the words ELIVES MAGIC SUPPLIES—S. H. ELIVES, PROP.

I could sure use a little magic about now, thought Justin. He glanced at his watch. Most of the stores in town were closed by this time of the evening. But this one had a light in the window.

He tried the door. It opened smoothly.

A small bell tinkled overhead as he stepped in.

Justin smiled. He would never have dreamed Barker's Elbow held such a wonderful store. Magician's paraphernalia was scattered everywhere. Top hats, capes, scarves, big decks of cards, and ornate boxes covered the floor, the walls, the counters, even hung from the ceiling. At the back of the shop stretched a long counter with a dragon carved in the front. On top of the counter stood an old-fashioned brass cash register. On top of the cash register sat a stuffed owl. Behind the counter was a door covered by a beaded curtain.

Justin wandered to one of the counters. An artillery shell sat there, thick as his wrist. To his disappointment, the shell had already been fired. Attached was a tag that said, LISTEN.

Remembering the big seashell his mother used to put to his ear so he could "hear the ocean," Justin lifted the empty metal shell and held the hollow end to his ear.

3

He could hear the sound of cannons and explosions, the terrified neighs of horses, the screams of wounded men.

He put the shell down. Quickly.

Next to the shell stood a French doll. When Justin reached for her, the doll blinked and cried, "Oooh la la! Touch me not, you nasty boy!" Then she began a wild dance. Justin pulled his hand back and the doll froze in a new position.

Deciding he should just *look* at the merchandise, he crossed to another counter. A broom resting against the edge blocked his view. Justin picked it up to move it out of the way.

The broom began to squirm in his hands.

Justin dropped it. He was about to bolt for the door when the owl he had thought was stuffed uttered a low hoot.

"Peace, Uwila," growled a voice from beyond the beaded curtain, "I'm coming!"

A moment later an old man appeared. He was shorter than Justin, with long white hair and dark eyes that seemed to hold strange secrets. His face was seamed with deep wrinkles. The old man looked at the boy for a moment, and something in his eyes softened. "What do you need?"

"I don't think I need anything," Justin an-

swered uncomfortably. "I just came in to look around."

The old man shook his head. "No one comes into this store just to look around, Justin. Now, what do—"

"Hey, how do you know my name?"

"It's my job. Now, what do you need?"

Justin snorted. What did he need? A real home. His mother and father back. He needed—

"Never mind," said the old man, interrupting Justin's bitter thoughts. "Let's try this. Have you ever seen a magician?"

The boy nodded.

"All right, then what's your favorite trick?"

Justin thought back to a time three years ago, back before his parents' accident. His dad had taken him to see a magician who did a trick where he locked his assistant in handcuffs, put her in a canvas bag, tied up the bag, put it in a trunk, wrapped chains around the trunk, and handed the keys to a member of the audience. Then he had climbed onto the trunk, lifted a curtain in front of himself, counted to five, and dropped the curtain. But when the curtain fell, the assistant was standing there, and the magician was inside the bag in the trunk. Justin had loved the trick, half suspecting it was real magic.

It had had a special name, something scientific.

"The metamorphosis!" he said suddenly as his mind pulled the word from whatever mysterious place such things are kept.

The old man smiled and nodded. "Good choice. Wait there."

Justin felt as if his feet had melted to the floor. The old man disappeared through the beaded curtain—and came back a moment later carrying a small cardboard box. Clearly it didn't have a big trunk inside. What, then? Probably just some instructions and . . . what? He was dying to know.

But he also knew the state of his pockets.

"I don't think I can afford that," he said sadly.

The old man started to say something, then paused. He looked into the distance, nodded as if he was listening to something, then blinked. His eyes widened in surprise. After a moment he shrugged and turned to Justin.

"How much money do you have?"

Though he was tempted to turn and run, Justin dug in his pocket. "Forty-seven cents," he said at last.

The old man sighed. "We'll consider that a down payment. Assuming the trick is satisfactory, you will owe me—" He paused, did a calculation on his fingers, then said, "three days and fifty-seven minutes."

"What?"

"You heard me! Now, do you want it or not?"

Something in the old man's voice made it clear that "not" was not an acceptable answer. Swallowing hard, Justin said, "I'll take it."

The old man nodded. "The instructions are inside. We'll work out your payment schedule later. Right now it's late, and I am tired. Take the side door. It will get you home more quickly."

Justin nodded and hurried out the side door.

To his astonishment, he found himself standing beside the tree once more. He would have thought the whole thing had been a dream . . . if not for the small cardboard box in his hands.

Justin walked home slowly. The later it was when he got there, the greater the chance his uncle would be asleep.

Luck was with him; Uncle Rafe lay snoring on the couch, a scattering of empty beer cans on the floor beside him.

Justin tiptoed up the stairs to his room. He set the box on his desk, then used his pocket-knife to cut the tape that held it shut. He wasn't sure what he would find inside; it was way too small to hold the entire trick. Probably he'd have to go out and buy the trunk and stuff, which would mean that he'd never get to try it.

The box contained two items: an instruction booklet and a silky smooth bag that—to his astonishment—shook out to be as large as the canvas sack the magician had used.

The colors in the fabric shifted and changed as he looked at it. It was very beautiful, and at first he was afraid that it would be easy to tear. But it felt strong beneath his fingers.

He opened the instruction booklet.

The directions were written by hand, in a strange, spidery script. On the first page were the words "WARNING: Do not attempt this trick unless you really mean it. Do not even turn the page unless you are serious."

Justin rolled his eyes . . . and turned the page.

The directions there were even weirder:

"To begin the metamorphosis, open the bag and place it on your bed. Being careful not to damage the fabric, climb inside before you go to sleep. Keep your head out!

"After you have slept in the bag for three nights, you will receive further instructions."

Justin stared at the bag and the booklet for a long time. He was tempted to just stuff them back in the box and take the whole crazy thing back to the old man. Only he wasn't sure he could find the store again, even if he tried.

He rubbed the whisper-soft fabric between his fingers. It reminded him of his mother's cheek.

He climbed inside the bag, feet down, head out, and slept. That night his dreams were sweeter than they had been in a long, long time. But when he woke he felt oddly restless.

Justin slept in the bag the following two nights, just as the directions said. In his dreams—which grew more vivid and beautiful each night—he flew, soaring far away from his brutal uncle and the house where he had felt such pain and loss. He came to long for the night, and the escape that he found in his dreams.

On the morning of the fourth day Justin felt as if something must explode inside him, so deep was his restlessness. Eagerly, fearfully, he turned to the instruction booklet that had come with the silken sack. As he had half expected, he found new writing on the page after the last one he had read—the page that had been blank before.

"Sometimes a leap of faith is all that's needed."

Wondering what that was supposed to mean,

he went to the bathroom to get ready for school.

His shoulders itched.

The next morning they were sore and swollen.

The morning after that, Justin Jones woke to find that he had wings. They were small. They were feeble. But they were definitely there.

He had two reactions. Part of him wanted to shout with joy. Another part of him, calmer, more cautious, was nearly sick with fear. He knew Uncle Rafe would not approve.

He put on a heavy shirt and was relieved to find that the weight of it pressed the wings to his back.

The next morning the wings were bigger, and the morning after that bigger still. He wouldn't be able to hide them from his uncle much longer.

The wings were not feathered, nor butterfly delicate, nor leathery like a bat's. They were silky smooth, like the sack he slept in. More frustrating, they hung limp and useless. Late at night, when his uncle was asleep, Justin would flex them, in the desperate hope that they would stretch and fill, somehow find the strength to lift him, to carry him away from this place.

*   *   *

Exactly one week after the first night he had slept in the sack, his wings became too obvious to hide. When he sat down to breakfast, his uncle snapped, "Don't slouch like that. Look how you're hunching your shoulders."

Justin tried sitting up straighter, but he couldn't hide the lumps on his back.

"Take off your shirt," said his uncle, narrowing his eyes.

Slowly, nervously, Justin did as he was told.

"Turn around."

Again, Justin obeyed. He heard a sharp intake of breath, then a long silence. Finally Uncle Rafe said, "Come here, boy."

Turning to face him, Justin shook his head.

His uncle scowled. "I said, come here."

Justin backed away instead. His uncle lurched from the table, snatching at a knife as he did.

Justin turned and ran, pounding up the stairway to his room. He paused at the door, then ran past it, to the attic stairs. At the top he pushed the door behind him and locked it.

A moment later he heard his uncle roaring on the other side. For one foolish moment Justin hoped he would be safe. Then the door shuddered as the man threw himself against it. Justin knew it would take only seconds for Uncle Rafe to break through.

He backed away.

Another slam, another, and the door splintered into the room. Stepping through, Uncle Rafe roared, "Come here, you little heathen!"

Shaking his head, mute with fear, Justin backed away, moving step by step down the length of the attic, until he reached the wall and the small window at the far end. His uncle matched his pace, confident in his control.

Justin knew that once Uncle Rafe had him, the wings would be gone, ripped from his shoulders. Pressing himself against the wall, letting all his fear show on his face, he groped behind him until he found the window latch. With his thumb he pulled it open, then began to slide the window up. It hadn't gone more than half an inch before his uncle realized what he was doing and rushed forward to grab him.

"Don't!" cried Justin, holding out his hands.

The wings trembled at his shoulders, and he could feel a strange power move out from them. His uncle continued toward him, but slowly now, as if in a dream. Moving slowly himself, Justin turned and opened the window all the way.

He glanced behind him. Uncle Rafe's slow charge continued.

Taking a deep breath, Justin stepped out.

He fell, but only for a moment. Suddenly the wings that had hung so limp and useless for the last few days snapped out from his shoulders, caught the air, slowed his fall.

They stretched to either side of him, strong and glorious, shining in the sun and patterned with strange colors. As if by instinct he knew how to move them. And as his uncle cried out in rage and longing behind him, Justin Jones worked his wings and flew, rising swiftly above the house, above the trees, his heart lifting as if it had wings of its own.

Justin flew for a long time, as far from Barker's Elbow and the home of his brutal uncle as he could manage to go. He changed course often, preferring to stay above isolated areas, though twice he flew above towns, swooping down just so that he could listen to the people cry out in wonder as they saw him. One time he flew low over a farm, where an old woman stood in her yard and reached her arms toward him, not as if to catch him, but in a gesture that he knew meant she wanted him to catch *her* up. He circled lower, and saw with a start that tears were streaming down her face. Yet when he flew away, she made no cries of anger as his uncle had, only put her hand to her mouth and blew him a kiss.

And still he flew on.

Though Justin had no idea where he was heading, he could feel something pulling him north, north and west. After a time a cloud appeared ahead of him. It was glowing and beautiful, and without thought, he flew into it.

The air within seemed to be alive with light and electricity, and as Justin passed through he felt a tingle in his skin—a tingle much the same as the feeling he had had just before finding the magic shop.

When he left the cloud, he had come to a different place. He had been flying above land when he entered it, a vastness of hills and forest dotted by small towns that stretched in all directions for as far as he could see. But though it had taken no more than a minute or two to fly through the cloud, when he left it he was above water—a vast sea that, like the hills and forest, stretched as far as the eye could reach. Panic-stricken, Justin turned to fly back. But the cloud was gone, and the water stretched behind him as well.

Justin's shoulders were aching. He wasn't sure how much longer he could stay aloft.

And then he saw it ahead of him: a small island, maybe two or three miles across, with an inviting-looking beach. The wide swath of sand gave way to a deep forest. The forest rose up the flanks of a great mountain that loomed on the island's far side.

With a sigh of relief, Justin settled to the beach. He threw himself face forward on the sand to rest.

Soon he was fast asleep.

When Justin opened his eyes, he saw three children squatting in front of him.

"He's awake!" said the smallest, a little girl with huge eyes and short brown hair.

"I told you he wasn't dead," said the largest, a dark-haired boy of about Justin's age. "They never are, no matter how bad they look."

"Come on, then," said the girl, reaching out to Justin. "Lie here in the sun all day and you'll get burned."

Justin blinked, then glanced back at his shoulders. The wings were still there. Why didn't these strange children say anything about them?

"Maybe I should just fly away," he muttered, pushing himself to his knees. He did it a little bit to brag, a little bit to see if he could get the children to say something about the wings.

"Oh, you can't do that," said the little girl, sounding very sensible. "Well, you could. But it wouldn't be smart. Not until you've talked to the old woman."

16

"She's right," said the boy. "Come on, we'll show you the way. But first you ought to eat something."

"So you've seen people with wings before?" asked Justin.

"Silly!" giggled the girl. "We all had wings when we came here. Were you scared when you went through the cloud? I was."

Justin nodded, uncertain what to say. He realized someone else seemed to be in the same condition. "Doesn't he ever talk?" he asked, gesturing to the middle child, a dark-eyed boy of about nine.

"Not yet," said the girl. "I think he will someday. But he was in pretty bad shape when he got here."

"Come on," said the bigger boy. "The old woman will tell you all about it."

Justin followed the three strange children up the beach and into the forest, a forest so perfect that it almost made him weep. It was not that it was beautiful, though it was. Nor that the trees were old and thick and strange—though they were. What made it so wonderful, from Justin's point of view, was that it was filled with tree houses, and the tree houses were filled with children. Happy children. Laughing children. Children who scrambled along rope bridges, dangled from thick branches, and swung from tree to tree on vines.

"Hey, new boy!" they cried when they spotted him. "Welcome! Welcome!"

No one seemed to think it odd that Justin had wings, though a few of them gazed at the wings with a hungry look.

Justin's own hunger, which he had nearly forgotten in the wonder of this new place, stirred when the children led him to a platform built low in a tree, where there were bowls of fruit and bread and cheese. He ate in silence at first, too hungry to talk. But when the edge was off his appetite, he began to ask questions.

"Ask the old woman" was all they would tell him. "The old woman will explain everything."

"All right," he said when his hunger was sated. "Take me to this old woman, will you please?"

"We can't take you," said the boy. "You'll have to go on your own. We can only tell you the way."

Justin walked through the forest, following the path the children had shown him. The trees were too thick here for him to spread his wings, which annoyed him, because the path was steep, and his legs were beginning to grow tired. He wanted to fly again. Where did this old woman live, anyway? A tree house, like the children? That didn't seem likely. Maybe a cottage in some woody grove or beside a stream? Maybe even a cave. After all, he did seem to be climbing fairly high up the mountainside.

It turned out that all his guesses were wrong. The path turned a corner, and when he came out from between two trees he found himself at the edge of a large clearing where there stood a huge, beautiful house.

The door was open. Even so, Justin knocked and called out. There was no answer.

Folding his wings against his back, he stepped through the door.

"Old woman?" he called.

He felt strange using the words instead of a name, but that was the only thing the children had called her.

"Old woman?"

"Up here!" called a voice. "I've been waiting for you, Justin."

He blinked, then realized that given everything else that had gone on, the fact that she knew his name should be no surprise at all.

Justin began to climb. He went up flight after flight of stairs, traveling far higher than the house had looked from the outside.

At each level he called, "Old woman?"

And at each level the voice replied, "Up here, Justin! I'm waiting for you!"

At last the stairs ended. Before him was a silver door. He put his hand against it, and it swung open.

"Come in," said the old woman.

She was sitting before a blue fire, which cast not heat, but a pleasant coolness into the room. Her hair was white as cloud, her eyes blue as sky. A slight breeze seemed to play about the hem of her long dress.

"Come closer," she said, beckoning to him.

He did as she said.

She smiled. "I'm glad you're here. Do you like your wings?"

Justin reached back to touch one. "They're the most wonderful thing that ever happened to me," he said softly.

The old woman nodded. "I'm glad. It's not easy getting them out there, you know. I can't do nearly as many as I would like."

"Who are you?" asked Justin.

She shrugged. "Just an old woman with time on her hands, trying to do a little good. But now listen carefully, I have to tell you what happens next. The wings will last for only one more day. However, that will be long enough for you to fly home, if you should wish."

Justin snorted. "Why would I want to—"

"Shhh! Before you answer, you must look into my mirror. Then I will explain your choice."

Standing, she took his hand and led him across the room. On the far side was a golden door. Behind it, Justin could hear running water. When she opened the door, Justin saw a cave. Four torches were set in its walls.

In the center of the cave was a pool. A small waterfall fed into it from the left. A stream flowed out to the right.

"Kneel," said the old woman. "Look."

Justin knelt, and peered into the water. He saw his own face, thin and worn, with large eyes where the fear was never far beneath the surface. From his shoulders sprouted wings, huge and beautiful.

The old woman dipped her finger in the water and stirred.

The image shifted. Now Justin saw not a boy but a man. Yet it was clearly his face.

"The man you will become," whispered the old woman.

Justin stared at the face. It was not handsome, as he had always hoped he would become. But it was a good face. The eyes were peaceful and calm. The beginning of a smile waited at the corners of the mouth. Laugh lines fanned out from the eyes. It was a strong face. A kind face.

Outside, far down the mountain, Justin could hear the laughter of the children.

The old woman stirred the water again. The man's face disappeared. The water was still and showed no image at all.

"Come," she said quietly.

Justin followed her back to the room.

"Now you must choose," she said. "You can stay here. This place is safe and calm and no one will hurt you, ever again."

He felt his heart lift.

"But . . . you will stay just as you are. Never change, never grow any older." She sighed. "That's the trade. There's always a trade. It's the best I can do, Justin."

He went to the window. It looked out not onto forest or mountains, but clouds. He stood there a long time, looking, listening. Finally he turned to the old woman.

"Can I ask a question?"

"Certainly—though I can't guarantee I will know the answer."

He nodded. "I understand. Okay, here's the question. The man I saw in the pool. Me. What does he do?"

The old woman smiled. "He works with children."

Justin smiled, too. "And what about my uncle?" he asked. "Will things be better with him if I go back?"

The old woman shook her head sadly.

Justin blinked. "Then how is it possible I can turn out the way you showed me? How can *that* be me?"

The old woman smiled again. "Ah, that one is easy. It is because no matter what happens, you will always remember that once upon a time . . . you flew."

Justin nodded and turned back to the window. Far below he could hear the children at play.

He ached to join them. But he thought of the others he knew.

The ones who never laughed.

The ones who still needed wings.

"How would I find the way back?"

"Take the side door," said the old woman softly. "It will get you home a little more quickly."

Tucking his wings against his back, Justin stepped through the door—and found himself on top of the mountain. He could see the entire island spread out below him. Even from this height he could hear the children.

He took a deep breath, then spread his wings and leaped forward. Catching the air in great sweeps, he soared up and up, then leveled off and flew.

Not toward home; Justin Jones had no real home.

Flexing his wings, he pointed himself toward tomorrow.

Then he flew as hard as he could.

Some people just can't keep their big mouths shut.

THE WORLD WHERE WISHES WORKED

Stephen Goldin

There once was a world where wishes worked.

It was a pleasant enough place, I suppose, and the people were certainly happy. There was no hunger in this world, for a man had only to wish for food to have it appear before him. Clothing and shelter were equally easy to obtain. Envy was unknown there—if another person had something that seemed interesting, it was only a wish away from anyone else. There was neither age nor need. The people lived simple lives, devoted to beauty and the gentle sciences. The days were a pleasant blur of quiet activity.

And in this world, there was a fool.

Just the one.

25

It was enough.

The fool looked about him one day, and saw that everything was the same. Beautiful people doing beautiful things amid the beautiful scenery. He walked away from the others, down to a private little dell beside a lily pond, overhung by graceful willows and scented with spring fragrance. He wondered what things would be like if something new or different were to be. And so he concocted a foolish scheme.

"I wish," he said, "that I had something that nobody had ever had before."

Only a fool could have made a wish like this, for he left the object of his desire completely unspecified. As a result, he instantly came down with Disease, which had hitherto been unknown. His eyes went rheumy and his nose went runny. His head ached and his knees wobbled. Chills ran up and down his spine.

"I dod't like this," he said. "Dot at all. I wish to cadcel my last wish." And he immediately felt well again.

"That was close," he sighed, as he sat down on a large rock beside the pond. "The trouble is that I don't think before I say things. If I thought things out first, I wouldn't get into so much hot water. Therefore: I wish I would think more before I do any more wishing." And so it was.

However, being a fool he failed to spot the fallacy of his logic: namely, that a fool will think foolish thoughts, and no amount of foolish thinking will help him make wise wishes.

Thus deluded, he began to think of what his next wish should be. He did not even consider wishing for wealth, since such a thing was impossible in a world where everyone had anything. Material desires were too commonplace. "What I should wish for in order to satisfy this new restlessness of mine," he thought, "is the rarest of all commodities. I wish for love."

A frog jumped out of the lily pond and landed *squish* right in his lap. It looked up at him adoringly with big froggy eyes filled with tenderness, and croaked a gentle love call.

"Yuk!" exclaimed the fool, and he instinctively scooped up the frog and threw it as far from him as he could. The pathetic little creature merely croaked sorrowfully and started hopping back to the rock to be with its beloved. Quickly, the fool canceled his last wish and the frog, frightened, leaped back into the pond.

"That was a foolish wish," evaluated the fool. "Most of my wishes are foolish. Most of the things I say are foolish. What can I do to keep from saying foolish things?"

Had he not been a fool, he would simply have wished to say only wise things from then on. But, fool that he was, he said, "I know. I hereby wish not to say foolish things."

And so it was. However, since he was a fool, *anything* he could say would be foolish. Consequently, he now found that he could say nothing at all.

He became very frightened. He tried to speak, but nothing came out. He tried harder and harder, but all he accomplished was getting a sore throat. In a panic, he ran around the countryside looking for someone to help him, for, without the ability to speak, he could not undo that previous wish. But nobody was about, and the fool finally fell exhausted beside a footpath and started to sob silently.

Eventually, a friend came along the path and found him. "Hello," said the friend.

The fool moved his mouth, but no sound escaped.

"I don't believe I heard you," the friend replied politely.

The fool tried again, still with no success.

"I am really not in the mood for charades," said the friend, becoming annoyed over the

fool's behavior. "If you can't be more considerate, I'll just leave." And he turned to go.

The fool sank to his knees, grabbed his friend's clothing, tugged at it, and gesticulated wildly. "I wish you'd tell me what the matter was," said the friend.

"I made a wish that I not say anything foolish, and suddenly I found that I couldn't say anything," the fool told him.

"Well, then, that explains it. I am sorry to say it, my friend, but you are a fool, and anything you say is likely to be foolish. You should stay away from wishes like that. I suppose you want me to release you from that wish."

The fool nodded vigorously.

"Very well. I wish you could speak again."

"Oh, thank you, thank you."

"Just be careful of what you say in the future, because wishes come true automatically, no matter how foolish they are." And the friend left.

The fool sat down to think some more. His friend had been right—anything he was likely to say would be foolish, and his wishes would automatically come true. If that were so (and it was), he would always be in trouble. He could remain safe by not saying anything—but he had just tried that and hadn't liked it at all.

The more he thought, the worse the problem became. There seemed to be no acceptable way he could fit into the system.

Then suddenly the answer came to him. Why not change the system to fit himself?

"I wish," he said, "that wishes did not automatically come true."

Things are tough all over.

Beauty is only skin deep.
Magic, on the other hand, goes right to your very
core.

TRANSITIONS

Nina Kiriki Hoffman

I was twelve when my sister Opal went through transition.

There were five kids in the LaZelle family, and Opal was the oldest.

Jasper, the next oldest, teased Opal for being timid and wimpy. She never dared a dare or took the lead in follow-the-leader. She didn't like walking to the Santa Tekla beach with us because the tunnel under the freeway was full of broken glass and spooky echoes. Small squirmy things frightened her. Caterpillars gave her nightmares! Even baby birds, with their near-naked skin and gaping beaks, unnerved her.

As for me, Gypsum, the middle sister, I

didn't lead, but I didn't back down from danger, either. I could run almost as fast and hit almost as hard as Jasper, and harder than Beryl, Flint, or Opal. I could sink more baskets than anybody. I had more fun playing with Jasper than with Opal, even though Jasper was bossy and Opal was nice.

I remembered how Opal used to hug me when I was little, and comb my hair, and rock with me in the big rocking chair and sing to me, but that was when I was three and she was seven. I got older and grew out of that stuff.

A lot of things changed when Opal went through transition.

We all expected to get the sickness in our turn. It was something every kid in our family went through, if they were lucky.

It didn't look comfortable. First Opal got the shivers, then she got the sweats, then back to the shivers. She moaned a lot, and sometimes she talked, but not about anything I could understand.

Mama did most of the nursing, but I helped. I kept blankets on top of Opal when she was cold instead of letting her shiver them off. I didn't always like Opal, but I loved her no matter what. Watching her eyes burn with fever in the dim light, I was scared. I didn't want her to die.

The power came on Opal at midnight of the third day. I was asleep by her bed. I woke to find her hand gripping mine, and when I looked at her, she smiled and blew me a kiss. I felt it melt into my cheek like sunlight.

After that, she was okay.

Her settling-in period was mild compared to some we'd heard about from Great-uncle Tobias, who was the family historian and our teacher in all the special family things we couldn't learn at public school.

Opal only had little spurts and glories as she and her gift adjusted to each other, not the pyrotechnics and major risks and accidents some people had to deal with.

When she figured out how to work her gift, she used it on Jasper.

Jasper had been her chief tormentor the past few years, though often he had gotten me to help him. We'd dropped a lot of worms and ice cubes down the backs of Opal's dresses, and scared screams out of her with numberless stupid tricks.

Opal wasn't scared anymore.

Every time Jasper relaxed, she would set something invisible in his path and trip him. He worked up an amazing crop of bruises.

When Opal got a little stronger, she took over Jasper's legs and walked him places he had no interest in going, like into the pool. He never knew when she was going to attack. He had trouble sleeping.

I remembered Opal used to have trouble sleeping when we spent all our time sneaking up on her.

Jasper came up with a plan. He made me stick with him, and when Opal took over his legs, Jasper would grab me and hang on. She never got strong enough to control two people at once, and she wasn't that mad at me, so after Jasper kicked me a few times while she was running his legs, she gave up torturing him.

For a while after that we didn't see Opal do anything flashy.

Great-uncle Tobias had told us that once you got the power, you had to use it somehow. People who didn't use their power got twisted up inside and generally died from some ailment or mishap. It had happened to Great-great-aunt Meta, who got the power of curses instead of the more common wish-power. She didn't know anybody she wanted to curse. Unused curses had turned to cancer inside her.

"What do you think Opal's doing with her powers anymore, Gyp?" Jasper asked me one day when he and I were in our fort in the middle of the bamboo thicket. It was cool and quiet and private there. All the light in the thicket was green, and the air smelled like sweet grass and wet earth. The floor was papered with long pale leaves.

Opal had grown up so much she never came to the thicket anymore. We used to all hang out there, hiding from our parents and the neighbor kids, making plans, but Opal had started changing even before transition.

"She must be doing something," Jasper said. "She's not choking up like Uncle Tobias said she would if she wasn't using her powers. What's she doing, Gyp?"

"You haven't been watching carefully enough," I said. I watched everything, particularly things I couldn't understand. If I studied them enough, maybe I could figure them out. "She's beautifying herself. She buys fashion magazines and studies them, then fixes her face different every day. She changes her eye and hair color, too, but only a little, so Mama won't get on her case."

"Trust Opal to do something stupid with her gift!" Jasper said.

"You weren't talking like that last month," I said. Last month Jasper had spent a lot of time in the pool with all his clothes on.

He gave me a look. I didn't talk back to him very often.

"I want to watch her do it," he said after a short silence that was supposed to teach me a lesson.

"All right." I liked spying on people. I figured I would be an anthropologist when I grew up, and they were the biggest snoops I ever heard of. "How?" As the oldest, Opal had her own room; the rest of us doubled up, me with Beryl, Jasper with Flint. Opal's room had big windows, but it was on the second story and not near enough a tree for us to climb up and see in.

"Let's hide in Opal's closet," said Jasper.

"Right before she has a date is the best time," I said. At sixteen, Opal was dating more than I planned to in my entire life.

Jasper and I listened to Opal at supper that night. Sure enough, she told Daddy she was going out Friday from five to eleven. She used to ask him about stuff like that, but no more.

I decided I wouldn't let transition take me that way, stop doing what Daddy said just because he couldn't force me to anymore. I would respect him after transition the way I did now, even though Daddy was an outsider and had no wish-power.

*   *   *

By four Friday night Jasper and I were in Opal's closet. He was mad when I told him we had to be there a whole hour before the date. "Trust me," I said. "She's going to take an hour." Luckily she'd already laid the dress for her date across her bed.

The closet smelled like violet sachet. I found it stifling.

Opal came into the room about ten past four, by which time Jasper was already mad at me and pinching. I had to pinch him back to get his attention. He peered through the keyhole, which left me without much of a view. We had left the door open a crack. A sliver of light laid a stripe across Jasper and a finger on the edges of a couple of the dresses.

"Does she change her looks before or after she gets dressed?" Jasper whispered. I leaned forward and saw the light from the keyhole shining in his eye.

"Let me look," I whispered. He frowned, but he moved. I watched Opal take off her school dress and slip into her date dress.

Then she sat at her mirror.

"What's she doing?" Jasper elbowed me aside and peered out the keyhole again.

Opal had asked for a dressing table complete with lighted mirror and ruffles last year, and even though Mama and Daddy never gave us big presents for Christmas, Opal got her dressing table. Maybe that was another part of growing up, but I would have asked for a ten-speed bike.

"Hey," Jasper said, almost a talk instead of a whisper. He sat back on the shoes. I peeked through the keyhole.

I could see our sister's face in the mirror, and already it looked less like her. She had wider cheekbones and a bigger mouth. She lifted a magazine and looked at a picture in it, then leaned toward her mirror and ran a thick brush over her face. In the track of the brush stroke, she changed back to her original self.

Jasper tugged at my shoulder then, so I backed away and he got the keyhole for the rest of the time. Opal made one trip to the closet for shoes, but she didn't see us because the shoes were right in front of the door when it opened, and we weren't.

When she left the room at ten minutes after five, Jasper and I went to look at that brush. "Yah HAH," said Jasper, picking it up, "do you suppose—?" He reached out and brushed my cheeks with it. He must have done it wrong, because they came out bright slick red, like a doll's. "Trust that dumb Opal to put the power in a brush instead of keeping it inside herself," said Jasper, and he painted my nose—green.

"Jasper Elliot LaZelle, you stop that!" I yelled, and jumped him. I was so sudden I grabbed the brush before he could stop me. I brushed brown in patches all over his face.

We had quite a tussle after that. He ended up with curly spiral horns, and I got black lips, and purple eyeshadow up to my eyebrows. I was trying to give Jasper an extra eye when the brush stopped working.

We broke apart, staring at each other and breathing hard. Like one person we got to our feet and looked in the dressing table mirror.

"That dumb Opal," said Jasper, tugging at his horns, which refused to budge. "She never has enough power to finish what she starts."

I rubbed my nose and cheeks, but the color was there to stay. I licked my lips. They remained black. I wondered for how long. "What are we going to do?"

"Wait till she gets home, I guess," said Jasper. "We sure can't let Mama see us like this." His face was patchy brown and green.

"You really think she'll help us after we used her brush without asking?" I couldn't imagine even goody-goody Opal being that nice.

"Maybe it's a short spell," said Jasper. "She never does things the hard way."

"But it's got to last at least six hours," I said.

"Oh, yeah. She wouldn't want to fall apart on her date."

We giggled, thinking about pieces of Opal dropping off on Robin. "There goes her nose," said Jasper.

"Oops! Lost her hair."

"Where's that winning smile?"

We were still laughing when I realized someone else was peering into the room. Luckily it was only Beryl. "What are you doing?" she demanded in an agonized whisper. "It's suppertime!"

Mama favored letting us settle our fights among ourselves. She told Daddy that was the way it worked in our family. I didn't think she would ignore this particular fight, though, especially since Jasper and I had broken a couple of important rules—don't go in somebody else's room without asking, and don't mess with their things ditto.

Jasper turned into his General self. "Beryl, we're going to sneak up to yours and Gypsum's room and stay there till this wears off. Tell Mama Gyp and I went to the Outpost for supper, and bring us up some food and maybe a deck of cards, okay? Or the Scrabble game, that'd be good."

"But—what happened to you?"

"We found out where Opal keeps some of her power," said Jasper. "Check and see if the coast is clear."

We got to my room with no trouble. Beryl said Jasper could lie on her bed if he let her touch his horns.

It was a difficult evening. Jasper was as restless as a whole hive of bees in flower time. Beryl said Mama and Daddy weren't happy that we had gone off without telling them about it, either. As the night wore on, Beryl came upstairs during the ads on TV and told us the parents were getting madder and madder. We were supposed to call plenty in advance if we wanted to make alternate supper plans.

Opal came home a little past eleven. Jasper and I had the bedroom door open to hear what was going on downstairs. Daddy had words with Opal for being late, mostly because he was mad at me and Jasper, but she wasn't in any mood for criticism. She stomped up to her room and, after she had been in there long enough to try her beauty brush, let out a shriek.

By that time Jasper and I were in *my* closet, a much tighter fit than Opal's.

"What if she can't take off her face-lift without the brush?" I whispered. "Maybe we'll never get rid of these faces!"

"They'll wear off," Jasper whispered back. "It's Opal, remember? Besides, I think permanent, lasting change feels different. You didn't feel changed all the way through when I painted you, did you?"

"No. Just surface." But what if I had to go to school Monday morning with red cheeks, a green nose, purple eyelids, and black lips?

I'd have to stay home sick. For as long as it took.

It was hot in my closet and Jasper and I were both sweating, but we didn't dare venture out until we changed back to ourselves.

"Jasper," I whispered presently, "are you going to get all weird when you go through transition?"

"Haw!" he said. "When I go through transition, things are going to change, you betcha. I'm not going to put my power in anything but me, for one thing. For another thing, Opal will never be able to get me again. I'm not going to blow my power on anything stupid like makeup, either. I'm going to do real stuff with it, mage stuff like figuring out how water runs or where the top of the sky is. And I'll practice turning people into things. What would you like to be?"

"A cat, I guess. You better not do anything much to me, 'cause I'll transition right behind you." I said that, and then I shivered even though I wasn't cold. What if I wasn't right behind him?

What if transition killed me?

What if transition killed Jasper? That would be worse.

Things stayed tense in the closet for the next hour, but around midnight I touched Jasper's forehead and felt that his horns had gone.

Getting loose of that spell was like getting out of prison. I felt such a lift in my heart, I didn't even care Saturday morning when Daddy sentenced me and Jasper to eight hours of extra chores for going out without telling and staying out past curfew.

Opal caught up with me later that day when I was folding laundry—usually her job.

"Did you go into my room last night?"

I couldn't look at her. Sometimes I could lie pretty convincingly, but right now I felt too wrong. We really weren't supposed to play with each other's things without asking.

I matched a pair of light blue socks and folded them in thirds.

"Gyp, tell me, and tell me true," Opal said, putting a pusher in it.

"Yes," I said.

"You played with my brush and made all the

power run out of it? Power it took me three days to store in it?"

"Yes."

She stood in the door of the laundry room, staring at me. Her regard lay across me like a weight.

"I'm sorry," I said. "I'm really sorry, Opal."

"From now on you're going to stay out of my things, Gyp. Next time you try anything like that, I'll make your changes permanent," she said.

I looked up at her and saw a new and scarier sister. Not just the sister who walked Jasper into the pool. A cold sister who didn't care if I hurt.

For a second I wished I was little again so she could sing to me about all the pretty little horses.

"One other thing," Opal said. I saw no trace of her child self in her. "Did you do it alone?"

I stared down at the jeans I was folding and didn't answer.

"It's all right," she whispered. "I know who did it. I'll get him."

Opal demonstrated that she finally knew how to get mad.

She sat Jasper down in a chair and paralyzed him. All he could do was breathe and blink.

"Think about this," she told him after she'd left him there for fifteen minutes. "Mess with my things again and I'll leave you like this for longer. Blink twice if you understand and promise not to do it again."

He didn't blink twice. Not right away, anyway. In fact, before he gave in, he got sick, and Mama made Opal let him go.

Tobias said it was transition sickness. Opal had been late to transition at sixteen; Jasper, fourteen, was at a normal age for it to take him.

I spent the next three days taking care of my brother, tipping water into his mouth whenever he would let me, sponging off his forehead when he got too hot, piling covers on him when he got too cold. Transition hit him a lot harder than it had hit Opal. He shivered so much he lost weight, and he was out of his head all the time. He yelled and thrashed and fought with things I couldn't see.

Even Mama was worried.

There was a time near the end of the third day when I got under the covers with him and hugged him hard because his skin was so icy and I didn't know how else to warm him up. "Don't die, don't die, don't die," I kept whispering to him, rubbing his arms and his chest and trying to stop his shivering. I knew I should have called down to Mama, but I didn't

47

even want to walk to the bedroom door. I was afraid if I lct go of Jasper his spirit would escape his body. I hugged him and chafed his skin and cried and wished somebody—anybody—would come and help me. "Stay here. Stay here. Stay here," I whispered to him.

When my throat was sore from talking and my arms were so tired and heavy I wasn't sure how much longer I could go on, Jasper hugged me. "It's okay," he whispered. I touched his forehead. It wasn't too hot or too cold. It was just right.

I fell asleep smiling.

When I woke up, Jasper was sitting up among the snarled, sweat-soaked blankets and shoveling hot Cream of Wheat into his mouth. "Want some?" he said.

I shook my head.

"You should eat, Gyp. I know you've been taking care of me. You haven't been getting enough food or sleep."

I rubbed my hand across my face. My skin felt greasy. "Are you okay?"

"Yeah. Starved is all." The cereal he was eating was steaming, but that didn't seem to bother him. He swallowed without chewing.

"Did the power come on you?"

He smiled down at me. "Oh, yes. Oh, yes."

He put the spoon down and drank the rest of the hot cereal, set the bowl aside and wiped his mouth with the back of his hand. "I need a shower, and then I need lots more breakfast. You want to sleep some more?"

I checked in. Every muscle in my body felt stretched and tired. I nodded.

He smiled again, sweet as an angel, and touched my forehead; and I fell into a deep, comfortable sleep.

Jasper and I sat in the bamboo thicket a couple days later. The sun was pounding down on the yard, but the bamboo shade was cool, even though no breath of breeze moved through the canes.

Jasper had had three accidents already—power surges that once shut off the electricity in the house for two hours, once did unfortunate things to most of the food popped popcorn, melted butter, burned bread, cooked eggs in their shells, baked apples in the fruit bowl, exploded milk and juice cartons all over the inside of the fridge—and once made all the paint in his room blister and peel off the wall in long twisted strips.

Flint and Beryl were afraid to be near Jasper. Mama and Opal and Tobias could channel power surges, so they weren't scared of him, just irritated.

A power surge could really hurt me, but I didn't care.

Jasper had tried to make me stay away from him. I wouldn't. Now he was holding a green stone I had found at the beach that morning, and staring down at it. He murmured a chant Uncle Tobias had taught him. I huddled on the papery white leaves, hugging my knees, and I watched my brother speak to a stone in a language I did not know.

"Keep this," he said at last, holding the stone out to me.

"Why?"

"It's got power in it. I know I said I wasn't going to do that, but you need this. It should protect you from power—mine, or Opal's, or anybody's."

I took the stone. It felt warm in my hand. I looked up at my brother. "I thought your going through transition was going to change everything for the better."

"I feel a lot different," he said.

"What does that mean?"

He stared over my shoulder, leaf-green light touching his eyes. "I don't know. I just—I can't imagine hiding in a closet to spy on Opal. I can't believe I did that just last week. There are so many more interesting things to do."

"Mage things?" I whispered.

He nodded.

"Things I can't do."

He licked his upper lip, then nodded again. He looked beyond me. "Everything's talking, Gyp. I couldn't hear it before, but now I can. There are voices everywhere. I have to learn their languages."

A minute went by before he met my gaze again. No wonder he had looked so distracted since transition.

I said, "Can you do a predictor mystery for me?"

"Which one?"

I set down the rock he had given me. I opened my backpack and pulled out a watch and a little zipped-shut bag of flower petal dust. This was something Uncle Tobias had taught us last fall. "Tell me . . ."

"What, Gyp?"

"Tell me when I'll transition. I don't like being on the other side of a wall from you."

"You really want to know?"

I thought about that. Tobias had told us to be careful of questions. Some would offer us answers that would hurt. I felt a chill brush the back of my neck. Then I thought, *Opal's sixteen, Jasper's fourteen, I'm twelve. Will my transition be soon? Will it be this year? Or will it be three years before I know what Jasper and Opal know now? If I have some idea of when I will transition, I can plan. Or at least I can stand it.*

What if I don't survive it? Do I want to know?

If I don't survive it, I better do a lot of things now.

"I want to know," I said.

Jasper took the spell ingredients from me and prepared them, then said the chant that would give us an answer. He tossed the flower dust up and watched it float down. I watched, too.

When Uncle Tobias had demonstrated Image in the Air, I had seen a picture of Mama as a young girl, which was what Uncle Tobias had asked about.

This time I just saw flower dust drifting, swirling down. Maybe only Jasper could see the picture. I looked at him.

"No," he whispered, shaking his head.

"No what?"

He hesitated. "No transition."

"What?" I felt like someone had punched me in the gut.

The dust settled. Jasper looked away. "I

could be wrong. I haven't tried this before. Maybe it's not one of my skills."

"What did you see?" I whispered.

"Nothing."

"What did you see?"

He shook his head.

"What did you see?" I asked him a third time.

"I just saw you, older, but without any magic, Gyp. You. Just you."

Some people never went through transition. People in our family always married outsiders. Sometimes outsider genes stopped children from having a magical heritage. I had never imagined it could happen to any of *us*.

"Really," Jasper said, "I don't know what I'm doing. I probably did it wrong."

I felt cold despite the hot still air of the afternoon. I hugged myself and shivered.

Opal had moved away, and changed into someone I didn't know and wasn't sure I liked.

Jasper had moved ahead, and changed into someone I didn't connect with in quite the same way as I used to.

I wasn't going to change.

The future stretched ahead of me like a dark corridor I would walk all alone. All those notes I had taken while Uncle Tobias was teaching us—I might as well burn them. There was no skill inside me. My family was no longer my family. Cold welled up in my stomach and my chest, traveling outward to my toes and fingers.

"Stop it, Gyp." Jasper picked up the green stone, grabbed my hand, and closed my fingers around the stone. "Hang on. Hang on."

The stone was warm. I pressed it to my breastbone and felt its warmth wash through me.

"See? You *can* do magic."

I remembered working Opal's beauty brush. Painting horns onto Jasper's forehead. No problem there. If somebody gave me an object with magic in it, I could work it.

"Tell me whenever the stone needs a recharge," Jasper said. "I'll take care of you. And nobody needs to know."

"Not even Uncle Tobias?"

"You don't have to tell him. Let's pretend we never did Image in the Air, okay? Let's pretend you never asked the question." He patted my shoulder.

I could pretend, but I couldn't deny that everything had changed. Jasper had never patted my shoulder before. He felt sorry for me now. I couldn't wish away the answer to my question.

I felt the warmth that came from the green stone, and thought, *Well, all right. If pretending is what it takes, I'll be the best pretender ever.*

"I don't know my range, anyway. Maybe I didn't look far enough ahead," Jasper said. "Maybe you transition later."

How old did I look? I wanted to ask. Then I thought, *Better if I don't know.* I had heard of late transitions, but they were even more dangerous than normal ones.

I touched my forehead with the green rock. Warm as sunlight. I looked at Jasper, and noticed that his nose looked a lot like Flint's nose, and like my nose. Opal's beauty brush could stroke away any resemblance we had on the surface, but Jasper and I had been together in her closet, together in my closet, together in the bamboo thicket a week ago, a year ago, three years ago. A thousand thousand memories connected us. A million memories connected me to everyone in my family. Whatever else happened, nothing could change that.

I slipped the green stone into my pocket. "Let's go run through the sprinklers."

Jasper smiled and said, "All right."

I like this poem for its very quiet kind of magic.

UNDER THE BRIDGE

Lawrence Schimel

I know a bridge out in the woods
That arches over a clear, quick stream,
Where elven children like to laugh and scream
And make faces at the troll who lives below.

I sit upon that bridge as well
And toss flower petals into the current.
A mortal child, I am more reverent
Of the river's quiet, whispering spell.

The petals never float away on the other side
And when I rise to leave, a present is waiting:

A necklace of fish bones
Or three polished river stones,
A long, white swan's feather,
Or, sometimes, my flowers, put back together.

56

Hidden deep in the past are the answers to so many fascinating riddles. What a great magic it would be to find the answers to a few.

WHAT THE DINOSAURS ARE LIKE

Deborah Wheeler

Wally's favorite place in the whole city, in the whole world, was the Dinosaur Hall at the Museum of Natural History. He knew all their names: *Brachiosaurus, Stegosaurus, Triceratops, Velociraptor* and especially, *Tyrannosaurus rex*. He'd stare up at them for hours, trying to imagine what they'd looked like when they were alive.

That was how Wally met Joel, who was what the other kids called a dweeb. His hair was a ratty fringe of no particular color, and he always wore these rumpled flannel shirts about half a size too small. Joel rocked back on his heels and tilted his head up, staring right through the opened jaws of the mounted *Tyrannosaurus*.

"That's an exceptionally fine specimen," Wally said. "The greatest killing machine the world has ever known."

"There's a—a recent theory that tyrannosaurs were scavengers—carrion eaters—rather than predators." Joel's watery blue eyes blinked hard behind his thick glasses.

"I still wouldn't want to meet one in a dark alley," said Wally.

"A few years ago they said dinosaurs were cold-blooded and stupid," Joel said, warming up. "They said they just walked off and left their eggs. Now they've got it the other way around. But who really knows?"

Wally sighed. "I guess *we* never will."

"Don't you wish you *could* know what the dinosaurs are like?" Joel seemed to know just what Wally was thinking. "Not a dream, not a painting, not a movie. But really know?"

Wally nodded. If you looked long enough and hard enough, you could imagine what used to be, a shadow of something so powerful that even a hundred million years couldn't wipe it out.

After that, Wally and Joel would meet at the museum every Saturday afternoon and stay until closing time. They were sitting in the museum coffee shop, eating rubbery hamburgers, when Joel asked, "Do you believe in magic?"

"Are you putting me on?" Wally said.

"It's not so far-fetched when you think about it," Joel answered. "A hundred years ago everyone thought you couldn't change gold into lead, but now that we know about subatomic particles and radioactive decay, we can make elements in the laboratory that never occur in nature. Einstein proved everything is relative. So why not magic?"

Wally leaned back on the cracked plastic bench and stared. It was the most complicated speech he'd ever heard Joel make. "What are you getting at?"

Joel lowered his voice and took out a battered book from beneath his flannel shirt. "Last summer, my folks sent me to my grandma's place in the country. I spent the summer up in the attic, reading the stuff I found in her old trunks. There were lots of sci-fi magazines . . . and this book."

Wally could almost smell the dust and hear the way the pages crackled when Joel turned them. The ink had turned brown, it was so old.

"I found this thing called 'A Window in Time,'" Joel went on, "and I wrote it down—"

"But you never tried it," Wally said.

"I couldn't. It takes two people . . . and this."

Joel reached into his shirt pocket. "I found it at a garage sale, stuff that belonged to this lady who used to tell fortunes."

Joel dropped a circle of hard dark clay into Wally's palm. It had been stamped with a design and then painted.

"See this symbol?" Joel said. "It's the exact same one as from the book."

Wally realized what Joel had in mind. "No way!"

"What have you got to lose?"

"We may be a couple of crazy kids, but we don't have to act like it."

"No one will find out if we don't tell them," Joel pointed out. "It's quiet, we can do it after hours. And the worst that will happen is nothing. We'll feel a little stupid, but so what? I'll buy you a soda and that will be that. But what if it works? Just think of it, Wally. *What if it works?*"

In the end, Wally said yes. Perhaps he was a little worried that if he didn't, he might start believing and wondering what might have happened. What could it hurt to try?

That night they hid in the rest room until after closing. The dim lights made the exhibits look softer, more like living bone and less like rock. Wally and Joel tiptoed into the Hall. It felt stuffy, like a swamp holding its breath.

Wally had never noticed how deep the eye sockets of the *Tyrannosaurus* were. His mind started playing tricks, imagining the eyes that had once glittered beneath the heavy ridges. He pictured them flickering, quick like a lizard's, scanning the ground for prey.

Kneeling on opposite sides of a large white candle, they held the amulet above the flame. Wally had to admit that what followed was impressive, with the candle casting eerie shadows over the mounted skeletons. Joel had said they must say their desire aloud. They'd argued over what era to choose—Joel wanted the Jurassic because his favorite dinosaur was *Stegosaurus*. Wally voted for the Late Cretaceous, when true giants battled to rule the earth. But if he got to see a real dinosaur, he didn't care.

Together they chanted the odd-sounding words which sounded as if he ought to know them, like *Abracadabra*, only not quite. Joel's voice rang out, "We want to know . . . what the dinosaurs are like!"

The air around the amulet shimmered, or maybe it was the heat from the candle. The old bones seemed to lean closer, listening.

Wally held his breath and waited.

And waited.

Nothing happened. Of course nothing happened.

"Well," Wally said when he figured they'd waited long enough. "That's it. I'm outta here."

Red-faced, they both let go of the amulet at the same time. It clattered on the tile floor and broke into two equal pieces. Joel slipped one half into his pocket and gave the other to Wally.

"I feel like such a dork." Joel put the candle out.

Wally patted him on the back. Under his flannel shirt, Joel's back was bone and gristle. "That makes two of us. Don't worry about it."

"Wally . . ." Joel stopped at the water fountain and glanced over his shoulder. His hands shook as he took off his glasses and wiped them with the end of his shirt. "I think—it's just that when you stare at them long enough, in this dim light and all—well, the bones seemed to move."

"Now you're seeing things!"

"I think we should give it a longer chance! What if it works but we've gone home? We'll miss it!"

Wally stomped over to the far wall, which is how he almost missed what happened next. He was standing beneath the *Lambeosaurus* replica, which was only a plaster model. It had never

been alive, and no magic could touch it. Then he heard something—a whisper of air, like wind moaning through shutters.

He held his breath.

"Wally?" came Joel's voice from the shadow of the *Tyrannosaurus*.

Silence. And then a creaking, like an old ship that has taken on too much water, bending until it breaks.

Wally could no longer make himself believe his eyes were playing tricks. Across the room the stones which had once been living bone swayed on their mountings. Iron rods shrieked in protest. In the middle of the room, something snapped.

Wally ran toward where he'd last seen Joel, circling in back of the *Stegosaurus*. As he passed, the tail whipped out, the heavy spikes rattling—*thump!*—as the thing came down inches from his leg. He froze.

Slowly the narrow skull swiveled toward him, pits of blindness where eyes once rolled. Air hissed through the arching ribs in a horrible imitation of breath.

From the twilight in the center of the room came a throat-tearing shriek. Something moved on the floor—Joel, on his knees and elbows.

Wally ran to Joel and scooped his hands under his friend's armpits. Then Joel's muscles went rigid and his fingers sank like needles into Wally's shoulder.

Wally turned his head and looked, too—looked up.

Twenty feet of carnivorous hunger. Saber teeth. A mouth that could swallow them both alive. *Tyrannosaurus* . . .

. . . standing there not even breathing, but Wally knew the thing was AWAKE, it knew they were there . . .

. . . warm bloody morsels to crunch and maybe a thrill at their scrabbling to escape but they'd never get out in time . . .

. . . NEVER you NEVER got away from him NEVER . . .

. . . the tyrant king . . . the bringer of death . . .

. . . the monster in the dark . . .

Wally screamed. He tried to back up and tripped over his own feet. Joel fell on top of him, but neither one of them could move, only stare at the red light flickering in the eye sockets, the jaws looming closer and closer until they blotted out all sight and sound. Wally felt himself being jerked away, tumbling alone through the darkness. . . .

Wally's eyes snapped open. He was standing at the edge of a pine forest.

Joel? Where are you?

The air tasted different, full of wild, outdoor smells. He straightened up and felt the shift of balance as his forelegs folded and his tail lifted.

His . . . tail?

Astonished, he glanced down at his new body, slender and agile, with a glossy scaled hide. He could hardly believe his eyes.

Wow!

He'd gotten his wish, all right—finding out what the dinosaurs are like. But he never dreamed it would be by becoming one!

To his left lay a field of flowers, lapping a mountain of shimmering gold. Sound flooded his ears, trilling cries above a deep bass melody which rumbled through his bones.

It lured him from the pine woods. With each gliding step, his clawed feet sent billows of scented pollen aloft, butterflies and lizards scurrying. Flowers brushed the underside of his belly. His tail swished through the strange coarse grasses.

He wondered where Joel was—some other place, some other era, still back in the museum?

As he drew near the golden mountain, he saw it was not, as it first seemed, a dome of smooth metal, but made up of tile or scales, like a mosaic, each tile delicately frosted with gold. The central mound, seven or eight feet high, rose and fell rhythmically.

It was *Tyrannosaurus rex*, in the flesh, lying on its back in a field of sun-drenched flowers.

Singing.

Its eyes were closed and its mouth open. Birds, or something very like them, perched along the massive hind legs and tail, while things that were small and dark-furred crept between the gaping jaws, picking between the teeth with their paws. In a circle around the tyrannosaur's four-foot-long head sat a choir of smaller dinosaurs. Wally was too stunned to remember their names, but most of them looked vaguely familiar, graceful creatures in mottled sorrel, or bright blue, armored and sleepy-eyed, a duckbill with little ones rubbing against her emerald-shaded flanks. They looked at him with unblinking eyes, and one by one they stopped singing.

You idiots! Wally thought. *Any moment now that thing will wake up and you'll be lunch!*

The birds took off in a flurry of squawks and flappings and the little dark ratlike things scurried into the undergrowth.

The *Tyrannosaurus* opened its eyes. Wally expected them to be golden like the monster's hide, dragon's eyes full of greed and deceit.

Under their overhanging eye ridges, they were the color of cinnamon.

Wally knew he should run away. Any moment now the giant carnivore would hunt him down for sport. Instead, a sense of calm filled him. The thing must be hypnotizing him, preparing to swallow him whole.

Instead, the *Tyrannosaurus* began to sing again. In the long, timeless-seeming afternoon, other singers joined it, including a ponderous *Triceratops* with one horn broken off halfway and its blue-gray hide laced with pale, knotted scars. They sang until a moist wind sprang up and the sky turned murky. Wally sank to his belly in the flowers and drank in the sound.

The *Tyrannosaurus* rolled to its feet and stood, tail extended and body almost horizontal. Then it lifted its tail and began to run like the wind. Wally darted after it. Soon it was lost to view, but he followed its footprints.

He caught up with the tyrannosaur along a cliff above a muddy riverbank. At the bottom, among the fallen rocks, a small hadrosaur lay on its side, its neck twisted. It had been a beautiful creature, gazelle-built with a hide like caramels in cream. Now its eyes were bloody sockets, and one side had been laid open to the bone. A pack of hyena-sized carnasaurs circled it, dashing in to slash off chunks of living flesh, while above, pterosaurs screamed as they hovered and dove.

The *Tyrannosaurus* let out a roar and suddenly the sky was empty, the carnasaurs yelping as they dashed upriver. Slowly it went down the bank and lowered itself into the mud beside the hadrasaur. Wally, huddling on the crest, could barely hear the tyrannosaur's hum. He felt it like a vibration in his bones, the aching sweetness. He, too, became part of the song, at one with every element of the endless, arching sky, the warm sun, the green fern-trees, even the coppery smell of blood.

The only movement was the ragged rise and fall of the hadrasaur's ribs. The tyrannosaur bent over its throat, and then the smaller dinosaur lay still, at peace.

The *Tyrannosaurus* sat back on its hind legs, its voice rising. Wally wished he could cry. Instead, he raised his head and opened his mouth, opened his heart, and sang along with the others.

Gradually the song changed even as the night sky brightened under the single bright southern star. The tyrannosaur climbed the bank. Its body blotted out the star. Below, the carnasaurs were already tearing at the hadrosaur's body. The tyrannosaur set off along the river, pausing often for Wally to keep pace with it, as if it were grateful for his company. Later, they slept.

Wally scrambled to his feet, for a moment puzzled that he was not in his bedroom. The sky was already light, a strange red-streaked yellow, more like sunset than dawn. He was surrounded by baby duckbills, honking and milling up against the tyrannosaur. He touched his shoulder to the golden hide for reassurance. The great beast hummed as it scanned the horizon.

Again came the rumbling, louder this time, and the rattle of panic-driven feet. A herd of *Struthiomimus* bounded by, beaks gaping for air. Several broke and ran for shelter beside the tyrannosaur, but the greater part hurried on toward the western darkness. More dinosaurs thundered past, a family of giraffe-spotted brachiosaurs and unrecognizable smaller creatures.

Without warning, brightness exploded across the sky, a wave of heat so dense it took Wally's breath away. The tyrannosaur jumped to its feet. Coughing, Wally stared at the wall of flame that raced toward them.

Wally froze in horror as he realized what was happening.

They were doomed, all of them.

That wasn't a star he'd seen last night, it was a comet—*the* comet, The Great Death Comet that had come hurling in from space and put an end to the dinosaurs. Some would die by fire, the rest from cold and starvation, as a thick black cloud covered the Earth. There was no place to run, no way to hide. Every single dinosaur—from the tree-tall brachiosaurs, *Triceratops* and *Velociraptor,* to the tyrannosaurs—would be gone forever.

The *Tyrannosaurus* let out the most blood-curdling scream Wally had ever heard. It was everything that had terrified him back in the museum, when the bones began to move and every nightmare became real. The great golden jaws loomed above him, snapping. His legs churned faster than he believed possible.

Then suddenly the ground fell away and he was falling, sprawling in the warm mud, flailing through the shallows and paddling frantically.

In the center of the slow-moving river, the water was cool and deep. Around him splashed other dinosaurs, crocodilians, even a few opossumlike mammals clinging to some branches. The water along the banks began to steam. On the bank, silhouetted against the leaping flames, stood the tyrannosaur. Its head was thrown back, nose lifted above the worst of the smoke, and, unbelievably, it was still singing.

Singing. Singing of peace and safety in the long sun-filled afternoons. Singing of perfect moments of stillness and harmony. Louder and louder it sang, above the hissing as the floating logs burst into flame and the fur of the opossums caught fire.

The trees on the far side of the river blazed and the banks on both sides were boiling. Some of the smaller animals had already lost consciousness from the smoke.

Between the billows of black smoke, Wally saw the tyrannosaur still standing on the bank. Louder and harsher it sang, not of peace now but of pain—pain that swallowed up all joy and comfort, pain that brought only mindless fear of more pain.

Wally's eyes sizzled. His lungs felt as if he had tried to breathe molten lava.

Get me out of here! Wally cried. *I changed my mind, I don't want to know what the dinosaurs are like! I want to go home!*

Agony drowned out the notes of the tyrannosaur's song. The steaming waters covered Wally over, and his bones sank into the mud.

There was no fire, no burning pain. His arms, his legs, his lungs, all firm and whole. Wally opened his eyes, already knowing where he was. In the museum, his museum, in the Hall of Dinosaurs.

"Joel?" he called. "I'm back."

There was no answer, only a faint echo. Wally got to his feet and brushed himself off. The broken amulet half was still in his pants pocket. He searched every corner of the room, went next door to the Hall of Mammals and the geology exhibits, covered every square inch of the museum, even creeping into the ladies' room. He found no sign of his friend.

Wally walked up to the *Tyrannosaurus* exhibit. He ducked under the cordon and climbed the little platform that housed the base of the armature. He laid his cheek against the cool fossilized bone and closed his eyes, listening with all his might.

The song was gone.

With a sigh, Wally turned to leave. It was then he noticed the new dinosaur. It was a small, complete skeleton, not much bigger than he was, mounted on its hind legs. He could have sworn he'd never seen it before. He came closer and saw the bluish light in its eye sockets, faint and blurred as if filtered through thick glass lenses.

Unknown species, Middle Jurassic, classification pending, the sign read.

Wally didn't know whether to laugh or to cry. Because Joel had found his way back to the dinosaurs, too, but millions of years before the comet, when the golden summer afternoons went on forever, and unlike Wally, he had chosen to stay. Somewhere back in time, a *Tyrannosaurus* was still singing . . . and Joel was singing with it.

*Wicked wizards have so many different ways
that they can be evil.*

THE WOODEN CITY

Terry Jones

There was once a poor King. He had a threadbare robe and patches on his throne. The reason he was poor was that he gave away all his money to whomever needed it, for he cared for his people as if each of them was his own child.

One day, however, a wizard came to the city while the King was away. The wizard summoned all the people into the main square, and said to them: "Make me your king, and you shall have all the gold and silver you ever wanted."

Now the townsfolk talked amongst themselves and said: "Our King is poor, for he has given all his money away, and while it is certainly true that there are no beggars in this kingdom, it is also true that none of us are very rich nor can expect to be as long as our present

King reigns." So at length they agreed that the Wizard should become their king.

"And will you obey my laws—whatever I decree?" cried the Wizard.

"If we can have all the gold and silver we ever wanted," they replied, "you may make what laws you wish."

Whereupon the Wizard climbed to the top of the tallest tower in the city. He took a live dove, and tore out its feathers, and dropped them one by one out of the tower, chanting:

Gold and silver shall be yours
And blocks of wood shall serve my laws.

Now that poor dove had as many feathers on its back as there were people in that city and, by the time the wizard had finished, everyone in the city had been turned to wood.

When the King arrived back, he found the gates of the city shut and no one to open them. So he sent his servant to find out what was the matter. The servant returned, saying he could not find the gatekeeper, but only a wooden mannequin dressed in the gatekeeper's uniform, standing in his place.

At length, however, the gates were opened, and the King went into the city. But instead of cheering crowds, he found only wooden people, each standing where they had been when the wizard cast his spell. There was a wooden shoemaker sitting working at a pair of new shoes. Outside the inn was a wooden inn-keeper, pouring some beer from a jug into the cup of a wooden old man. Wooden women were hanging blankets out of the windows, or walking wooden children down the street. And at the fish shop, a wooden fishmonger stood by a slab of rotten fish. And when the King entered his palace, he even found his own wife and children turned to wood. Filled with despair, he sat down on the floor and wept.

Whereupon the Wizard appeared, and said to the King: "Will you become my slave if I bring your people back to life?"

And the King answered: "Nothing would be too much to ask. I would become your slave."

So the wizard set to work. He ordered a quantity of the finest wood, and took the most delicate tools, with golden screws and silver pins, and he made a little wooden heart that beat and pumped for everyone in that city. Then he placed one heart inside each of the wooden citizens, and set it working.

One by one, each citizen opened its wooden eyes, and looked stiffly around, while its wooden heart beat: tunca-tunca-tunca. Then

each wooden citizen moved a wooden leg and a wooden arm, and then one by one they started to go about their business as before, except stiffly and awkwardly, for they were still made of wood.

Then the Wizard appeared before the King and said: "Now you are my slave!" "But," cried the King, "my people are still made of wood, you have not *truly* brought them back to life."

"Enough life to work for me!" cried the wicked old wizard. And he ordered the wooden army to throw the King out of the city and bolt the gates.

The King wandered through the world, begging for his food, and seeking someone who could bring his subjects back to life. But he could find no one. In despair, he took work as a shepherd, minding sheep on a hill that overlooked the city, and there he would often stop travelers as they passed to and fro and ask them how it was in the great city.

"It's fine," they would reply, "the citizens make wonderful clocks and magnificent clothes woven out of precious metals, and they sell these things cheaper than anywhere else on earth!"

One night, however, the King determined to see how things were for himself. So he crept down to the walls, and climbed in through a secret window, and went to the main square.

There an extraordinary sight met his eyes. Although it was the dead of night, every one of those wooden citizens was working as if it had been broad daylight. None of them spoke a word, however, and the only sound was the tunca-tunca-tunca of their wooden hearts beating in their wooden chests.

The King ran from one to the other saying: "Don't you remember me? I am your King." But they all just stared at him blankly and then hurried on their way.

At length the King saw his own daughter coming down the street carrying a load of firewood for the wizard's fire. He caught hold of her and lifted her up and said: "Daughter! Don't you remember me? Don't you remember you're a Princess?"

But his daughter looked at him and said: "I remember nothing, but I have gold and silver in my purse."

So the King leapt on to a box in the main square and cried out: "You are all under the wizard's spell! Help me seize him and cast him out!"

But they all turned with blank faces and replied: "We have all the gold and silver we ever wanted. Why should we do anything?"

Just then, the wizard himself appeared on the

steps of the palace, arrayed in a magnificent robe of gold and silver, and carrying a flaming torch.

"Ah ha!" he cried. "So you thought you'd undo my work, did you? Very well. . . ." And he raised his hands to cast a spell upon the King. But before he could utter a single word, the King seized the bundle of firewood that his daughter was carrying and hurled it at the wizard. At once the flame from the wizard's torch caught the wood, and the blazing pieces fell down around him in a circle of fire that swallowed him up. And as the fire raged, the spell began to lift.

The King's daughter and all the others shivered, and the tunca-tunca-tunca of their wooden hearts changed to real heartbeats, and they each turned back into flesh and blood. And when they looked where the wizard had been, there in his place they found a molten heap of twisted gold and silver. This, the King had raised up on a pedestal in the main square, and underneath he had written the words:

WHOEVER NEEDS GOLD OR SILVER MAY TAKE FROM HERE.

But, do you know, not one of those townsfolk ever took a single scrap of it as long as they lived.

I wonder if it's still there?

With her hilarious Enchanted Forest Chronicles,
*Pat Wrede has made an art form out of
turning fairy tales on their heads.
Here she is to do it again, in a shorter form.*

THE CINDERS CASE

Patricia C. Wrede

Explain why I want to transfer? That's easy:
It's because of the clients. Kids these days have
no respect for tradition, and as for gratitude,
well, you'd swear they never heard the word.

It used to be that when I showed up with a
couple of walnuts full of dresses like the sun,
moon, and stars, or a pair of ruby slippers that
take you home when you click the heels, I'd
at least get a "Thank you, good witch" or
"That's just what I wanted, godmother!" Nowadays—well, the next-to-last girl wanted a pair
of ruby combat boots, if you please, and she
was downright rude to me when I told her they
wouldn't suit a sweet pretty young thing like

her. Said I didn't understand modern fashions. And this last one . . .

That's right, the Cinders case. That's what her family called the girl—Cinders. The background file was quite normal: wealthy merchant family, mother dead of fever, father remarried to a woman with daughters of her own, father dead in a shipwreck, prince holding a ball . . . you know the sort of thing.

When I arrived, the client was out in back of the mansion, sitting on the steps and sniveling into a towel. She was quite startled when I popped out of a cloud of scented blue smoke.

"Who are you?" she asked. She was cleaner than I had expected, and not quite so pretty as they usually are, and her hair was an unfortunate dishwater-blond. Still, I was sure that the right clothes and a little fairy dust would take care of everything. It always does.

"I am your Fairy Godmother," I said, "and you *shall* go to the ball!"

She blinked, and unfolded herself up off the steps, and I got my first real shock. The child was *tall*, all elbows and legs and awkward angles. As for her feet—well, it was going to take some fancy enchantments to get the slippers to work. Size ten, at least, and as wide as . . . well, wide. Still, a bit of challenge now and then keeps one on one's toes. I was trying to decide what sort of gown would do the best job of hiding the girl's flaws when she said, "But I can't go. Stepmama—"

"Nonsense!" I said. "I know you haven't a dress or a coach, but that's why I'm here."

"But Stepmama is—"

"Your stepmother will never know," I said as kindly as I could. "Obedience is all very well, my dear, but sometimes you must follow your heart."

At that exact moment the rear door of the house flew open. "Cindy? Cindy!" said the auburn-haired girl in the doorway. "Oh, there you are. Mama wants some more lemon tea, and I can't find the honey jar."

"Cinders," my client corrected gloomily. "Not that it matters now."

I was horrified. Not just because the stepsisters were clearly still at home—though I must tell you that I had never before arrived at a client's home too early. But this girl was everything my client wasn't: tiny, graceful, and as lovely as an angel. The job was taking a difficult turn, but as I said before, a little challenge now and then keeps things interesting.

Then the auburn-haired girl saw me and hesitated. "Excuse me, ma'am. I didn't mean to interrupt."

Polite, too, I thought. *Still, a certain amount of challenge once in a while . . .*

"This is, um—" my client started.

"I'm an old friend of her mother's," I said.

"Pleased to meet you," the girl said, and then her eyes narrowed. She studied me for several seconds before she added, "*Very* pleased to meet you, actually. I don't suppose you'd come talk to my mother for a few minutes?"

"I don't see the need," I said firmly.

"Oh, please! She's sick in bed with a perfectly awful cold, and she won't let any of us go to the ball without a proper chaperon. It's bad enough for Abby and me, but Cindy—I mean, Cinders—has worked so hard for this, it's just not *fair* that she should lose her big chance."

"It's too late," my client said gloomily. "They were supposed to start five minutes ago."

The girl in the doorway stamped her foot. "It is *not* too late! Have you ever known them to get set up on time? Go get your things while I take this lady up to see Mama. If you leave now, you'll just make it."

"But if Stepmama says no—"

"She won't," the second girl said confidently. "I mean, just *look*. Have you ever seen anybody half so respectable in your whole life?"

86

They both turned to look at me. It was flattering, in a way, and I couldn't help straightening up. The standard blue silk godmother's uniform is quite grand, of course, but I think my diamond and sapphire necklace is the finishing touch. I always wear it when I'm working; I like to make a good impression. Judging from their expressions, I had succeeded.

"*Rich* and respectable," the auburn-haired girl said with satisfaction. "Mama will love it. What are you still doing here, Cindy—I mean, Cinders? Go, go!"

My client gave me a frantic look and bolted through the door. The auburn-haired girl shook her head fondly. "And she forgot to tell me where the honey jar is. You don't mind, do you, ma'am? Mama just doesn't understand; she thinks it's some sort of stage that Cindy will grow out of. If she wasn't so sick, I'd swear she caught this cold on purpose, just to keep Cindy away from the palace tonight."

I'd almost been feeling out of my depth, but this sounded more like what I was used to. *My client must have seen the prince out riding in the street and fallen in love*, I thought. *And naturally the stepmother wants him for one of her own girls, instead.* It was a bit unusual for the stepsisters to help out, but no doubt they were soft-hearted girls, and carried away by the romance of it all. So I nodded, and the stepsister led me inside.

The interview with the stepmother went rather well, even though I couldn't give her a piece of my mind the way I wanted to. She quickly agreed to let me chaperon her girls—*all three of them*, I made very sure she was clear about *that*—and I left the room feeling quite smug.

The feeling didn't last long. The second stepdaughter was waiting in the hall, and she was, if anything, lovelier and more graceful than the first. "Fran, what is going on?" she asked the girl beside me. "Cindy just came tearing through and said she was going after all, and could she borrow my silk blouse with the black lace sleeves, and then she grabbed the rest of her things and took off in the pony cart. Did you make her go anyway, or what?"

"Sort of," the girl beside me said. "This lady is a friend of Cindy's mother's, and we've fixed it up with Mama that she'll chaperon all of us at the ball. I just sent Cindy on ahead. This is my sister Abigail," she added for my benefit.

"So I guessed," I said dryly.

Abigail's forehead wrinkled charmingly. "But, Fran, if you've sent Cindy off in the pony cart, how are *we* going to get to the palace? It's too far to walk."

Fran blinked. "I hadn't got that part figured out yet," she confessed, and looked at me hopefully. "I don't suppose *you* have a coach handy?"

I was tempted simply to say *no*. My client's chances would be much better if I kept these two at home. On the other hand, she had gone off to the ball almost totally unprepared—no magic ball gown, no glass slippers, and no fairy dust. One way or another, I had to get to the palace and correct that, and I could hardly leave the two stepsisters behind at this point. I sighed. "Where do you keep your pumpkins?"

They looked at me as if I were mad, but the elder girl—Fran—said, "I don't think we have any, unless Mama still hasn't thrown away the jack-o'-lantern we carved for Halloween."

I swallowed hard. Jack-o'-lantern! A bit of challenge now and then is all very well, but there ought to be *some* limits. "I'll make it do," I said with another sigh. "Bring it out front, and bring a couple of mice from the mousetrap, while you're at it."

"Mousetrap?" the second girl said doubtfully. "I don't think there is one, and anyway, Mama had the exterminators in last week."

She would, I thought. "Come up with something else, then," I snapped.

"You find the jack-o'-lantern, Abby," Fran

said. "I'll take care of this other. Five minutes, at the front door."

I'll say this for them, they were quick. Four and a half minutes after I left them in the hallway, Abby turned up with a grinning jack-o'-lantern. Fran was hard on her heels, carrying two gerbils in a small cage. "Will these do?" she asked, holding it up.

I looked at them with distaste. "They'll have to. Set the pumpkin by the curb, and leave the cage in front of it, then stand back."

They did as I told them. I shook my wand out of my sleeve, then took another look at my starting material and almost stopped right there. But I thought of my client, hustled off to the palace in who-knew-what sort of gown, and I stiffened my resolve. Resisting the impulse to cross my fingers, I muttered the spell and waved the wand.

For a moment, I didn't think it was going to take. Then a cloud of blue smoke rose around the pumpkin and the gerbils, and I relaxed. I shouldn't have. When the smoke cleared, what stood beside the curb was a shiny hearse, harnessed to a pair of black mules. Mercifully, there was no coffin.

"Wow," one of the girls breathed softly from behind me. "Wait until Annie sees *this*. She'll like it even better than Ginny's black satin wedding dress with the spiders on the skirt."

I should have been grateful that the sisters hadn't the taste or sensitivity to object to riding in such a dreadful turnout, but at the time all I could think was that I was going to have to ride in it myself. Once that spell has been cast, you're stuck with the results until midnight.

The two girls climbed into the back, and I looked around for a rat or lizard to do for a coachman. There weren't any, and I was about to climb into the driver's seat myself—I've had to do that a time or two, though it isn't widely known—when a large brown dog shoved through the neighbor's hedge and barked at me.

"Ajax!" said Fran. "Stop that!"

The dog looked at her, and I quickly waved the wand again. A moment later an enormous young woman in a brown velvet coachman's uniform stood in front of me. She looked more like a wrestler than a coach driver.

"Oh, good heavens," I said, staring. "How— I mean, I thought your name was Ajax."

"It is," the young woman said. "Do you have some problem with that?"

"Ah, no," I said. "If you'll just drive us to the palace . . ."

"I suppose." She sauntered over and climbed

into the driver's seat. The mules rolled their cycs at her nervously. I came out of my daze just in time to scramble into the back before she cracked her whip. The hearse started off with a jerk, and I fell against the side. The stepsisters were at least polite enough not to laugh.

The moment the hearse pulled up at the palace gate, Fran leaped down and demanded of the footman, "Have they started yet?"

"They're just now playing the opening march, miss."

"Oh, good," Fran said. "I *told* her they'd start late."

"You girls go on in, while I have a look round for your stepsister," I said. I wanted to find my client before anyone saw her in whatever getup she'd worn. First impressions are so important.

Fran blinked at me. "But, Cindy—I mean, Cinders—will be in the main ballroom with the band. Where else would you look for her?"

I should have known, I thought with a strong sinking feeling. *My client has some silly crush on one of the musicians, and these two are helping her so that they'll have a better chance at the prince. Well, I'm not having it.* I squared my shoulders and marched into the palace and through the ballroom doors.

The opening march had just finished, and a

cluster of groupies stood around the band, shifting and squirming and generally behaving badly. From what Fran had said, I was certain that my client was among them, but I couldn't see her at first, though you'd expect anyone that tall to stand out above the crowd. Then someone called out, "Now that tradition is satisfied, let's have some *music!*" The groupies cheered and flowed out onto the dance floor, and I spotted my client at last.

She stood at the front of the band, her hair pulled back inelegantly and tied at the nape of her neck. Her long legs looked even longer than before in tall black boots and green leggings, and her face was intent. In one hand, she held a fiddle; in the other, a bow.

Of all the things I'd expected or feared, this hadn't even been on the list. No prince would overlook it, no matter how much fairy dust I used. My client had ruined her chances, and I couldn't do a thing about it now. If I hadn't let myself be distracted by stepsisters and jack-o'-lanterns, I told myself, it never would have happened. . . .

And then my client raised her bow, tapped her foot once, twice, and one-two-three-four, and began to play. The rest of the musicians came in with her, right on the beat. They were good, I had to give them that, and my client was the best of the lot. The fiddle swooped onto the melody and carried it off, and the dancers were carried right along with it. You could hardly help yourself. There was magic in that fiddle, or perhaps in the music or in the fiddle player—it was hard to tell which, even for me.

Beside me, Fran gave a happy little sigh. "Isn't she good?"

"Yes, but—"

"She's wanted to play in public for a long time, but Mama didn't approve. She only let Cindy audition this time because the band would be playing for the prince's ball, and she didn't think Cindy would have a chance. *I* knew she would come in first, and of course, she did. That's when she thought of using 'Cinders' as a stage name. But then Mama caught that cold, and . . . well, you know the rest. I'm so glad it worked out."

You might have told me, I thought, but there was no point in upbraiding the girl now. Abby nudged her sister, nodded once toward the dance floor, and ran down the stairs to join the whirling throng. Fran lingered a moment longer to thank me and then she, too, was off. Feeling numb, I made my way down the steps and slowly crossed to the punch table.

I had *never* failed an assignment before, but

I could see no way of salvaging this one. For the sake of a few hours in the limelight, my client had thrown away her entire future. She had no hope now of making a respectable marriage, and there was nothing I could do about it. Nothing.

Three cups of punch only made me feel more numb than ever. I didn't even flinch when Fran spun past in the arms of the prince. I did notice that the dance floor was packed, whether the fiddle rollicked or wailed or wept. Dance after dance, no one stopped moving for more than a few minutes. I hoped it would be enough for my client, once she realized what she had done.

I had just picked up my fourth cup of punch when the musicians paused for a break. I wandered toward the band—at that point, I had nothing better to do. They were surrounded by well-wishers, some of whom were clearly old friends and others of whom were, equally clearly, encroaching mushrooms. After a moment, Fran saw me and came over.

"Do you know that person who's talking to Cindy?" she demanded. "He's trying to get Cindy to sign some sort of exclusive contract, and I'm sure it would be a bad idea. I mean, he doesn't look to me like anyone who has clout in the music business, no matter what he *says*. Don't you think so?"

I barely glanced at the man. "He looks like an encroaching mushroom."

"That's what I thought," Fran said. "And Harold—that's the drummer—says some talent scout is supposed to come hear the band later, and maybe offer them a really good gig, but—"

"A gig?"

"A job playing somewhere. But if Cindy has already signed something, it won't work out. Or at least, it'll be a lot more complicated. And I don't trust that man. Can't you do something?"

I squinted at the man in question. His hair was greasy and he was wearing a plaid shirt. He had one arm draped over Cinders' shoulders, though he had to reach up a bit to do it. "I certainly think I had better do *something*," I said, waving my punch cup.

That was what gave me the idea, though possibly the first three cups of punch had something to do with it as well. I looked at the man once more, very hard, and stirred the punch three times counterclockwise with my right ring finger. Then I made my way to my client's side and addressed myself to the mushroom.

"I don't believe we've met," I said. "I'm

Cinders' godmother, and her chaperon this evening. Do have some punch."

The mushroom mumbled "Pleasetameecha" and took the punch. To do so, he had to remove his arm from my client's shoulders, which in my opinion was a very good thing. "You have a fine little musician here," he added, and took a swallow of punch.

"Mr. Overdon wants to be my manager," Cinders said. "For a standard ten-percent deal, he can get me all kinds of professional gigs. Maybe even opening for a big-name band!"

"How nice," I said. "What, exactly, is a 'standard ten percent deal,' Mr. Overdon?"

"She gets ten percent, I get the rest," the mushroom replied promptly. My client's eyes widened, and I smiled in satisfaction. There aren't many people who can do a really first-class truth spell on the spur of the moment, if I do say so myself.

"That isn't what you said a minute ago!" Cinders said, frowning. "Is that really standard?"

"It is for me," Overdon said, and laughed.

"And just what sort of professional gigs would my goddaughter be getting in return for ninety percent of her earnings?" I asked politely.

"Mostly playing in bars. I know a dozen

places that will pay top dollar for novelty acts—and a girl fiddling in a bar would be a novelty, believe me."

Cinders looked properly horrified. I smiled again. "I think they're about to begin playing again, Mr. Overdon. Why don't we discuss this elsewhere?"

"But she hasn't signed the contract," he objected hazily.

"We can't hold up the music," I said, and steered him away. As we left, I looked back over my shoulder and said to my client, "In the future, get some advice before you deal with people such as Overdon. I'm quite sure that some of your fellow performers would have warned you about him, had you asked them."

Cinders nodded and fell back to the safety of the band. I guided Overdon to a quiet niche hidden by a large potted palm—every ballroom has a spot or two like that. A few minutes later the music began again and I wandered back into view, leaving a very fat, confused rat blinking and waddling in circles on the floor behind the palm. It seemed the appropriate thing to do.

Cinders and her band were a big hit at the prince's ball. The prince himself asked them to come back and play for the next state ball. The talent scout turned up just before midnight; he was much impressed, and booked the group for a large festival the following month. None of us got away until two in the morning, but for tunately we all fit into Cinders' pony cart, so the lack of the jack-o'-lantern hearse was not a problem. Ajax was asleep on the porch of the house next door when we arrived home, and was considerate enough not to bark and wake up the neighbors, though I did not quite like the way she looked at me when I climbed down from the pony cart.

I heard later that the group did so well at the festival that they landed a tour gig, opening for some famous band of which I had never heard. So my client appears to have some sort of future ahead of her after all. Fran got engaged to the prince the week after the festival, but refused to set a date for the wedding until she finished her schooling. And I had to go through a disciplinary review—the first in my entire career—because my client had not married the prince. I squeaked by without a reprimand solely because of the happy ending clause. Cinders and the prince are both very happy with the way things turned out, so there wasn't much the review committee could say.

But now perhaps you understand why I'm applying for a transfer. I've had quite enough of trying to help young people and then having them insist on doing things their own way; I'd like to try the other end of the business for a change. I've already thought up some dandy curses, and after everything I've been through it will be a positive pleasure to turn some of those stubborn children into toads.

I love trees. But after reading this tale I may think twice before I sit down under one to rest again.

INTO THE FOREST

Alice DeLaCroix

Night had fallen when the girl stumbled into the forest.

Innocent of witchcraft, she had run as fast as fear could carry her, trying to escape her captors. She pressed her damp cheek against the rough bark of an oak tree, then sobbed her relief as she heard the pounding horses pass by, not entering the woods. Her pursuers were not as brave as she—or as desperate—for many were the tales of folk who'd not come out once they'd gone into this dread place.

Taloned bird feet gripped thick black branches; a dark wind tossed boughs heavy with long needles. The girl's heart beat wildly as she listened to the whine of the wind. She slumped to the ground, her legs gone rubbery, and curled her thin frame into a cradle of thick roots at the foot of a huge oak.

Heavy weariness sped her toward sleep, but just as quickly she was wide awake. "Aiee—!" Her scream was cut short as a violent force grasped her body and sucked her, whole, into the tree. The hollow, rooty mouth echoed a bone-crunching sound.

Among the roots the moist stink of dirt pressed against the girl, and she held her breath. "Phohh!" she gasped, then, and discovered there were small air pockets from which she could breathe. Earth and bends of root held her trapped, but before total panic could grip her, she was drawn upward, helpless as a ragged leaf in a whirlwind.

In the black interior of the tree, far blacker than the night forest had been, she sensed she was now upright, with space for movement. She squeezed her eyes closed—it was less terrifying than the wide-eyed blackness—and reached out.

Her hand met a solidness—wood, she could only guess. Moving slowly across the surface like an insect searching with feelers, her hand found bumps. Some kind of canker, or . . . or . . . "Uck!" The pustules broke open, spewing a smell so vile she recoiled, slamming her back into another wall. She lurched away from it, madly brushing at whatever was wriggling slimily against her bare neck, through her hair. Worms? Spiders?

"Let me out! Get me out of here! Oh, please . . ." Her fists pounded the wood.

But in another second she was being pressed from all sides. Painfully squeezed and pushed, as if she were being digested. She felt herself rise, farther, higher through the tree's insides.

Now something dripped onto her. Icy cold. Onto her head, off her nose, down her back. Drip, drip. Water, just water, but so different from being in rain. The smooth wood of her cage slipped by as she slowly rose, her dress sodden against her aching, bruised body. She pushed and clawed as best as she could, searching for an opening, an escape. If only she could discover a way out. There must be a hole; she mustn't miss it.

As she rose, the space around her narrowed. The walls of the tree now tightly surrounded her and became tacky to touch. The first dabs of molasseslike stickiness globbing down gave warming. The girl gulped as deep a breath as she could just before being pushed headfirst into thick, moving sap. She felt herself being coated like a taffy apple.

She was more helpless than ever, her arms

glued to her sides, her eyes sealed shut, her mouth locked against screaming.

And now, she couldn't breathe at all. Couldn't breathe. Couldn't . . .

Dawn seeped into the forest. The birds began chirping and flew from the branches.

"Dear," said the oak's mate with a soft rustle. "What bothered your sleep so? You moaned and groaned all night long."

"Oh!" the tree answered, shuddering at the memory. "I dreamed I swallowed a girl. What a horrid nightmare!"

What would a book of magical stories be without a unicorn? Of course, it's unlikely you've ever read about a unicorn quite like this.

SINGING THE NEW AGE BLUES

Margaret Bechard

Andrea Stanford called me the day after school let out for the summer. "Hey, Steve," she said. "I have a job for you. A pet-sitting job."

Ordinarily I would have hung up on her. Andrea Stanford is the biggest snob at Forest Haven Middle School. And I had no idea why she would call *me* about anything. But I really needed a new back tire for my bike. "How much are you paying?" I asked.

"Twenty bucks. In advance. It's just for a few days. You'll hardly have to do anything."

"Sure," I said.

I had to walk to her place, because of the back tire. It took me almost forty-five minutes to get all the way up the hill to the big houses at the top of Peachtree Estates. Andrea seemed really glad to see me. Almost like she'd been waiting out on the driveway the whole time. "Snowdrop's in the backyard," she said.

If the Stanfords had had a dog or a cat, I would have been surprised. Or even one of those fat, ugly little pigs. A unicorn didn't surprise me at all.

Snowdrop was lying in the middle of a big expanse of bright green lawn. He was about the size of a big dog, with lots of long white hair. His horn stuck straight up from his forehead. It was really kind of pretty, all rainbow colors, like an oil slick on a wet driveway.

Just to show I wasn't a total feeb, I said, "I thought unicorns were extinct."

Andrea shrugged. "You have to know where to get them." She glanced up at the windows of the house, looming behind us. "I'll get you Snowdrop's stuff. We'll only be gone for a week."

She loaded me up with a big checkerboard bag of Unicorn Chow, a food dish, and, finally, the end of Snowdrop's leash. Before I knew it, I was back out at the end of the driveway. "So," I said, "I'll see you in a week?"

"Or two. Don't call us. We'll call you." She stuffed a twenty-dollar bill into my hand. She took

off into the house, without even giving Snowdrop a pat goodbye.

The curtains were open in an upstairs window. While I watched, Mrs. Stanford sort of
danced by. Her hair was all loose and long, and
she looked like she was maybe still in her
nightgown. She had a little drum tucked under
one arm, and she was beating on it. It almost
sounded like she was singing, too. Suddenly
Andrea appeared at the window. She slammed
it shut and jerked the curtains closed.

I looked down at Snowdrop. He was staring
and staring up at that window. He had really
weird, pale blue eyes. Almost human-looking
eyes. I gave the leash a yank. "Come on, Bud.
You're with me."

We didn't exactly have a big, bright green
lawn in our backyard. Dad had paved it all
over, after Mom moved out, so he'd have more
room to work on his truck. I clipped the end
of Snowdrop's leash to Barney's old chain. Barney was our Rottweiler. We had to get rid of
him after he attacked Mr. Turner's Miata.

Snowdrop just kind of stood there, in the
middle of the truck parts, looking at me with
those creepy eyes. I filled the food dish. He
ignored it. I found an old hubcap and filled it
with water, but he ignored that, too. He just
kept standing there, staring at me. I reached

out to pat him. He dropped his head and then, suddenly, lunged straight at me. I leaped back, and the horn grazed my arm. "Stupid unicorn," I said, and I went into the house.

The radio was blaring out Dad's favorite song, "You Drove Your Eighteen-Wheeler Right Straight into My Heart." Dad was pulling a couple of He-Man dinners out of the oven. He slapped them down on the table. "Meat loaf or chicken?"

"Meat loaf," I said. I sat down and pulled the plastic off the top.

Dad was fishing two forks out of the pile of dirty dishes in the sink. He wiped the forks on his jeans, tapping his foot and singing along to the music. Then he glanced out the window. He stopped singing and tapping.

I braced myself. I knew he wasn't going to be too thrilled about having a unicorn in his backyard.

But he just shook his head. "That," he said, "is the plug ugliest dog I have ever seen."

I called Dougie O'Reilly after dinner, and we made plans for the next day. Once I had my bike fixed, the summer could really begin. Before I left in the morning, though, I figured I'd give Snowdrop a little treat. I dug around in the fridge and found a couple of floppy carrots, stuck to the back shelf.

Dad was already out back. He was wearing his "Oh, baby, baby" boxers and his emu-skin cowboy boots. He was pouring Lucky Charms into a bowl. "Watch this," he said. He poured milk onto the cereal. Snowdrop stuck his nose in and started eating. Dad laughed. "That's the third bowl he's eaten."

"You know, that may not be good for him," I said. "All those preservatives and stuff." Snowdrop raised his head and looked at me. A red marshmallow was clinging to his lower lip. I held out the carrots. He snorted and dipped his head back into the Lucky Charms.

"He doesn't eat salad," Dad said. He grabbed the carrots and tossed them over the fence into the Turners' yard. Mrs. Turner peeked over the fence, but she ducked back down when she saw us. Dad looked up at the sky and scratched his stomach. "Good day to change the oil," he said.

I gave Snowdrop more food and water Saturday morning, even though he hadn't touched the stuff he already had. And then, I was having such a good time riding around with Dougie, I forgot all about the dumb unicorn. Until Sunday afternoon.

I came home kind of late. Dad was sitting on the couch, drinking beer and watching the

111

truck pull on TV. The unicorn was sitting right beside him.

"Dad," I started.

He put up his hand. "Don't worry. He's housebroken." Dad leaned forward and poured some beer into a bowl on the floor. "He loves Coors," he said. As if to prove it, the unicorn lapped up a little of the beer.

"Dad," I said again. "What if he gets sick?"

"He's not going to get sick." Dad thumped Snowdrop's side, just the way he used to thump Barney. "Good for him. Puts hair on his chest." He laughed, and the unicorn put back his head, and he made this noise, kind of like a whinny, I guess, but it really sort of sounded like he was laughing, too.

By the time Andrea's week was up, the unicorn was waiting at the front door when Dad got home from work. It was sleeping at the foot of his bed. And it was eating cereal out of a bowl in the middle of the kitchen. I spent all day Thursday expecting Andrea to call. And thinking it was going to be kind of fun to tell her that her fancy-schmancy unicorn liked beer and Lucky Charms. Only Andrea didn't call. I reminded myself that she'd said maybe they'd be gone two weeks.

Dougie and I were spending a lot of time hanging out at the mall and cruising the park.

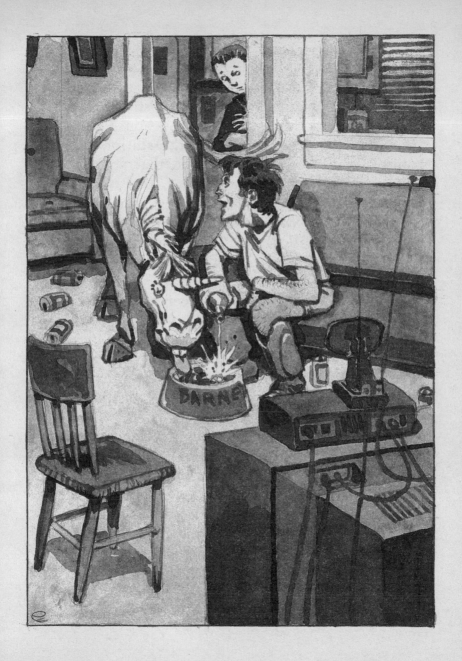

So maybe that's why it took me a little while to catch on. And it was just little things at first. Dad showering every day and slicking his hair back. And going around the house barefoot. And tuning the radio to the station that only played the new-age music that sounded like wind chimes.

On Wednesday night, I saw Dad coming out of the Crystal Empowerment and Self-Actualization store in the mall. I told Dougie he'd probably thought it was a bar. The next night a woman named Maya came over. She cooked dinner, a whole bunch of brown and green stuff, tossed together in the blender. She said it would brighten my aura. It sure wasn't He-Man meat loaf. Dad asked her for the recipe. And later she and Dad and the unicorn went into the living room, and Maya channeled an ancient Druid priest.

On Monday Dad went shopping. He bought himself baggy white pants and white shirts, and he filled the fridge with tofu and the cupboards with wild rice grown by Aztecs. On Tuesday he signed both of us up for a drumming class, a chanting class, and a class on how to build your own sweat lodge. He said I was spending too much time at the mall with Dougie.

114

I started calling Andrea four or five times a day. By Wednesday night I'd left about two zillion messages on her machine.

The wind chimes woke me up early Thursday morning. I went down to the kitchen, but nobody was there. The DJ on the radio whispered, "That, fellow wanderers, was 'Seascape in the Wind.'" I clicked the radio off.

Dad was outside, talking over the fence to Mrs. Turner. The unicorn was snuffling around his bare feet. Dad turned and headed back toward the house. He had a funny look on his face. If it had been anybody else, I would have said he was thinking.

He turned the radio back on as soon as he came in. It sounded like exactly the same song. Snowdrop bobbed his horn to the music. "Did you know," Dad asked, "that Mrs. Turner thinks she may have been an Egyptian princess in a past life?"

"Mrs. Turner?" I laughed. Mrs. Turner outweighed Dad by fifty pounds, and she always wore a Montreal Canadiens jersey. "They couldn't even fit her inside one of the pyramids!"

Dad frowned. "Steve. Remember. We're all just cosmic travelers." He smiled. "Besides, we were thinking maybe we knew each other before. Back in ancient Egypt. I think Mrs. Turner may have been my mother." There were tears

Margaret Bechard

in his eyes. He pulled me close and hugged me. "Wouldn't it be great to have Darlene as your grandma?"

Over his arm I could see Snowdrop staring at me. I pulled myself free. "Dad? Do you get the feeling something weird is going on here?"

But he was pouring himself a glass of breakfast out of the blender. "By the way, I called the guys at the garage and told them I'm quitting." He sighed. "Work was getting in the way of my astral projection exercises." He headed off into the living room, carrying his glass and a bowl for the unicorn. As Snowdrop passed me, he tossed his head. The tip of his horn caught my sleeve and ripped a big hole in my shirt. "Hey!" I slapped at him, but he was already out of reach, following Dad into the living room.

Two days later Dad sold the truck. The next day he gave away the TV and the VCR. "We need to simplify." He smiled at me. "Imagine how you could focus your energy if you didn't have that bike to distract you."

I rode straight to the Stanfords' house. Andrea opened the door. "What do you want?" In the living room I could see Mrs. Stanford. She was talking on a cellular phone, yelling about investments or something. Her hair was pulled

116

back tight against her head. She was wearing a black suit and high heels.

"You know what I want, Andrea," I said.

She grinned as she reached into her pocket. She pulled out a Nordstrom's credit card. "Mom reopened my account the day after you left." She started to shut the door.

"You've *got* to take the unicorn back."

She laughed, a nasty laugh. "Unicorns are extinct, dummy." And she slammed the door.

When I got home, Dad and the unicorn were in the living room. I couldn't help but notice that the CD player and the couch were gone, too. Big pillows were scattered around the floor. Dad was wearing his white pants and shirt. He looked like he was in his pajamas. He had a little drum tucked under his arm, and he was drumming and dancing and singing.

I went over and shut the curtains. Snowdrop was lying in the middle of the floor. He turned his head and looked at me. His mouth curved up in a little smile.

I went into the kitchen. It was really clean. I had to admit, it was nice to always have clean dishes. In the living room, the singing and drumming got louder. I dug out the school directory. I couldn't call Dougie or somebody I liked. I couldn't call anybody I was going to see very often. I needed a kid on the other side of town.

I dialed Tommy Marchetti's number. "Tommy," I said, "this is Steve Harper. I have a job for you. A pet-sitting job."

One should never ignore love's call. On the other hand, one should be careful when one answers.

VERNAN'S DRAGON

John Gregory Betancourt

Once, long ago, lived a girl named Sia. This was in the age of magic, when all things knew their true names and the twelve gods still walked the Earth.

Now it came to pass that on her twelfth birthday, Sia felt herself drawn to a quiet part of the river by her home. There, on that morning, magic shimmered over the water like millions of tiny rainbows. Sia knelt on the bank and sang an ancient song of love to her reflection. Legends told how girls might glimpse the face of their future love in these waters, and Sia longed to see hers today.

The water rippled with the falling of a leaf, and when the pool grew still again, Sia found herself gazing at a man. It was he who would be her husband. Staring at his handsome face, with deep blue eyes and golden-blond hair, Sia sank to her knees and continued to sing. The waters began to change, clearing to show a beautiful city bedecked with flowers and dazzling silk ribbons.

Sia recognized it at once, for surely there could be only one such city in all the land—Thelir, that place of wonders beyond all compare, where dwelt the immortal king Vernan. Sia knew she would find her husband there.

Weeping silently for joy, Sia looked up to see the golden sun break over the distant mountains. A redbird flitted overhead, piercing the springtime silence with bright song. The pool returned to normal; the magic ended.

King Vernan was a powerful wizard as well as the ruler of Thelir, and he worked the many spells and incantations needed to keep his people happy and prosperous. That did not leave him much time for his own pleasures, but he managed an hour or two of reading every week.

With the coming of spring, he took his leisure on a private balcony. As he sat there, studying one of his many books of ancient spells, the air suddenly filled with steam. He slapped

the book shut to keep the pages from being ruined.

The dragons were playing in the moat again. This was not permitted, and he knew he should tell them to stop. He didn't, though. He moved inside and let them continue. It was, after all, almost Festival. They could play in the moat just this once.

Sia returned home from the pool, bade her mother, father, and sisters good-bye, climbed onto her donkey, and set off for Thelir to find her future husband. He would be there. Magic never made a mistake.

When, after a long journey, she arrived at that great city, she found a wild Festival in progress. Her donkey slowly picked its way through the groups of dancers, jugglers, singers, and other Festival-goers.

"What is happening here?" she asked a woman selling sausages from a small cart.

The woman looked up in surprise. "Don't you know? Tonight is the night King Vernan will take a bride."

Everyone had heard of King Vernan, even as far away as where Sia and her family lived. He was immortal, it was whispered, and he took a wife every hundred years. Suddenly Sia knew that she would be his next bride.

A hush grew over the townspeople, and all strained their necks toward the sky. A dull vibration, like the thunder of distant hooves, grew steadily. From all mouths there came a gasp, for there, up in the sky, flew a chariot pulled by mighty winged horses, and in that chariot stood King Vernan.

The horses descended slowly, landing in a narrow place the men and women had cleared near Sia. Vernan smiled softly at her and held out his hand.

"Come be my wife," he whispered, but his voice was like thunder.

Sia said nothing, but walked forward, took his outstretched hand, and stepped into the chariot beside him. Vernan clicked to the horses, who spread their wings and bore them swiftly upward over the cheering crowds.

Later that evening, after the wedding and the Festival had died down, Vernan led his new wife into the castle garden. Distantly he heard the dragons still playing in the moat.

"My love," he said as he kissed her gently on the forehead, "your life is but a second when compared to mine, for I am immortal. Yet I love you as I have loved few others. I can give you the gift of eternal life, if you will accept it, and we will be together forever."

"Yes, my love," Sia whispered.

Vernan spoke the words, and the change was done.

"I truly love you," he said as he looked into her sad brown eyes. Laying his hand gently on her glistening scales, he stroked her long neck. "Now go and play with the rest of the dragons."

*In high school I was a social nerd—which
meant I didn't find out how much fun it was to
dance until long after I should have.
I still can't believe how much fun I missed
out on.
Of course, you can have too much of a good
thing. . . .*

BLUE SUEDE SHOES

Michael Stearns

I can't dance.

"Oh, bosh," my mother says, and she tells me
that I'm just self-conscious, that no thirteen-
year-old can dance. Then she lowers her paper,
peers at her watch, and says, "You're barely a
teenager. You've got plenty of time. Who cares
if you can dance?"

A good point. Mom always has a point—
she's a lawyer, and they pay her to have
points—but she really has a point about
dancing.

What good is dancing, anyway? Who needs it? You can't waltz out of algebra, can't box-step your way past Dead Bolt's fists in P.E. The Charleston won't get you into college, and you'll never rumba your butt into a good job. The jitterbug and the tango and the fox-trot and all the rest of them won't save your life or even bring back your dead dog or your dad from wherever he's gone. Dancing is good for nothing.

Good for nothing, that is, except for attracting girls. Or, more specifically, a girl. One very *specific* girl: Miranda.

Miranda isn't the prettiest girl in the eighth grade, and she isn't the most popular, and she isn't the smartest. But she may be the nicest, and I know for sure she is the only student who is passionate about something: dance.

Miranda dances. Three days a week she comes into sixth period in these tight legging things, her hair a blond knot on her head, silky white slippers waiting in her bag. And at the bell she flows out the door and across the school lawn to her mother's waiting car, and from there, to her three o'clock ballet class.

I know because I asked her about her clothes once. "What's with the fancy getup?" I asked. I was trying to make small talk.

She gave me this hurt look and said, "There's no time to change before my dance class." And then, as if I was stupid or something, she added, "I'm a *dancer*."

I haven't seen her dance, but I know she must be beautiful, curving and bending and twirling to classical music that I don't even like. I think about her as I walk home (run, if Dead Bolt spies me), think about how tall she is and how wonderful she looks when she moves. When Miranda simply walks across the room to write on the board, she moves like I wish I could move. Her whole body lights up with something—grace, I guess. Some adults move like that, but I . . . I'm a knot of knees and elbows when I try to do anything—bike, walk, get up to go to the bathroom—let alone *dance*.

I told as much to my aunt. I've gone to her with all my problems ever since my dad moved away.

"Oh, dear," Auntie Kay said. "You've got it bad, Matt."

"Got *what* bad?" I didn't feel sick, but adults are always better at noticing those kinds of things. I palmed my forehead.

"Got it bad for this *girl*. You're what, eleven?" She rolled back her wheelchair and shook her head. Auntie Kay is really my great-aunt, my mother's mom's sister, and she is older than just about anyone. But what's important is that my aunt knows dancing, and she knows romance. Auntie Kay has been married four times! The photos of her favorite husbands hang on her walls, and in at least three of the pictures she is dancing, one arm flung out, the other held by a dashing guy in a tuxedo. She looks airy and happy and above it all. Those photos are from long, long ago, before the accident with her feet.

"Thirteen," I said. "I'm thirteen."

"Old enough, I suppose," she said. "It's too bad my lessons never took."

Years before, my Auntie had tried to teach me to dance as she had taught my mother, when my mom was still a girl. It was a family tradition. There was still a confusing litter of dance steps and names in my head—the foxtrot, the mambo, the Charleston, the waltz—but the lessons just never worked out. Maybe it was because these days Auntie Kay was in a wheelchair. Or maybe it was because I am about as coordinated as a car wreck. Or maybe it was because I had no one to dance with. My mom just never had time for that sort of thing after she and Dad divorced.

Auntie Kay muscled her chair toward the back of her house. "I've got just the thing for you, Matt." She called out over her shoulder,

"You have *tried* going to dances, haven't you?"

Of course I've tried. I've been to dances—well, *a* dance. Back when I was younger.

I was eleven, and the teachers forced us sixth graders to go to this fancy-pants function in the cafeteria. Mrs. Moore and Mr. Vyse had transformed the cafeteria. They'd draped the walls in colored bunting and done weird stuff with the lights, and they'd even dropped a mirror ball from the ceiling. It would have been spooky and cool except that we were supposed to be out on the floor *dancing*.

Us guys all hung back against the wall by the doors. I think Alvin Turble and his gang were thinking of escape, but there were teachers stationed at each set of doors like wardens. If you went up to them, they just pointed and said, "Dance!"

So we danced. It was my first and only time. The song was some sort of disco thing with drums and screaming that sounded like a crowd being machine-gunned. I took Lori Davison's hand, and she and I went out to the center of the floor with the other couples, and then I did my thing.

Let me be clear. I have the *energy* to dance. But I don't have the moves. And dancing is all about moves. And coordination. If there is one thing I've never had, it is coordination. But I tried anyway.

I spazzed. I pistoned my arms, shot them up and down like I was climbing a ladder. I pivoted, I kicked, I wagged and wiggled and swung my rear around and hopped all over the place like I had to go to the bathroom. And I tripped people and fell all over the floor. Lori vanished sometime during my performance, and when I stopped to look for her, I noticed everyone had cleared a space around me. Above, thousands of points of light spun off the mirror ball and flowed along the walls, and I followed them with my eyes, spinning on my heel, until I got so dizzy I fell to the floor.

Two of the male teachers carried me out. "Nice moves," one of them sneered, and the other teachers laughed and laughed. At me.

"So yeah," I told my great-aunt now, "I've danced. I was terrible."

She rolled back into the room with a shoe box on her lap. "Well, those days are over, Matt my boy." She held the box out to me like it was a gift.

Right away I knew something was weird. It wasn't just that the box was dustier than my math teacher's brain. Or that it was made out of wood instead of cardboard. But when I grabbed the box, my feet tingled. Just a little bit. As though they'd been asleep because I'd sat on them wrong or something.

"They're Terrence's old blue suede shoes," Auntie Kay said.

"Terrence?" I asked. Auntie Kay had a million names in her head; they're hard to keep straight.

"My first husband." She got this glazed look on her face and sighed. "He was suave . . . the smoothest dance partner I ever had."

I asked for tips, and she gave me a stinky old pair of shoes. "Gee thanks, Auntie Kay," I said.

"Don't get snotty," she said, and she pried open the lid of the box. "These aren't just shoes, these are dancing shoes."

They may have been dancing shoes, but they looked pretty dorky to my eye. They were kind of like loafers, except they were made out of this soft blue leather—suede, in case you can't guess—and the heels were wooden. The toes were really stupid, though: They curled up like an elf's shoe in a bad movie.

"So he, like, wore these things?"

She laughed. "Of course. We won dancing contests with these shoes. I had a pair of red shoes that were twins to these, sort of, but . . . I had to get rid of those years ago." Her hands shot up off the armrests of her wheelchair and grabbed my wrists, and she leaned forward, all intense and frightening. "I was stupid back then, Matt, and cared more about being a great dancer than I did the people I danced with. Promise me you won't ever let the shoes make you lose sight of your partner. Never choose the shoes over a person."

"Yeah, whatever," I said, and tried to pull away. "Look, I don't care about the shoes; it's Miranda I'm interested in." I made my voice go all soft and sensitive, like Mom does when she's telling me I can't do something. "Nothing personal, Auntie, but I need tips on how to dance, not a new pair—an *old* pair—of dancing shoes."

"With these shoes, Matt, you don't need to know how to dance. The shoes know."

"What?" I said, and I went cold as I realized that my Auntie's wheels had finally lost a few spokes. "Like I suppose they're magic, right?"

A smile broke on her face and she let go of my hands. "Oh, yes. A magic the likes of which you don't see in the world anymore."

Just how desperate does a guy have to be to show up at his first eighth-grade dance wearing goofy shoes? Well, let me tell you, the shoes didn't fit. They were loose on my feet, as though this Terrence guy wore a size fifteen or something. I had to wear five pairs of socks just so they wouldn't fall off when I walked.

People noticed. All the wrong people noticed. The middle-school gym had been turned into the bottom of the ocean for the dance, blue lights and big paper fish, silly stuff. Dead Bolt was there, and he rolled up to me first thing and said, "Matt, nice shoes. Did Santa bring you 'em?" And then he stamped down with one of his fat feet.

Dead Bolt weighs more than just about any mountain on earth, and when his foot hit my toe it was like an avalanche. Everything dinged and went white around the edges, and my head went hollow with pain.

And then the disc jockey spun the first record, and something happened. I can't explain it. There was an electricity in my feet, in my legs, riding up my body and cracking my spine like a bullwhip. "Dead Bolt!" I bellowed.

He leaned away. "Door Matt?"

Next thing I knew, I had a fistful of Dead Bolt's shirt, and I was pulling him down a few feet, to my level, and in a gravelly voice not my own, I told him, "You can do anything, but don't you step on my blue suede shoes!" And then—and it scared me even as I did it—I shoved him. The push was nothing much, but it was enough to make him lose his footing and slide away on his big round rear.

And then I started dancing. Or I guess the shoes started dancing; I was just along for the ride.

I don't remember what song was playing, but it had a heavy bass thump to it, a ta-ta-ta-*boom* that sent the shoes into a strut across the cafeteria floor. With each *boom* my rear swung to the right or the left, the opposite leg shooting out, my arm leaping out, and a "Hey!" forcing its way from my throat. I shimmied my way around the dance floor once like this and then worked into the center, where I crossed my arms, dropped down on my haunches, and kicked my feet out in a blur, like some kind of crazy Russian. I had moves now, but they were all the wrong ones.

People laughed.

I blushed, even while yelling out "Hey!"

And then that song was over and something slower was playing, some sort of sappy love song like the ones my mother cried over. Some of the guys and girls hung on each other and did that swaying thing that passes for dancing. But not me, no, I found myself waltzing—I *think* it was a waltz; whatever it was, I was doing this complicated whirling step that drew me forward along a diagonal, until I was standing in front of Miranda.

She looked a little scared. "A waltz? You're *so* funny, Matt," she said.

"Miranda!" I gasped. "Dance?" I whirled.

"Maybe later," she said. "We can glam slam when something faster comes up." She laughed and shook her head. Then this guy minced up and took her hand, and they went out onto the floor and swayed together.

In grief, I spun away.

It was like that all night.

I danced by myself. I danced with a coat that someone threw at me. Once, inspired by a drumroll in some lousy song, I danced a soft-shoe along the length of the refreshment table, ending with a handstand and triple somersault at the far end. Everyone applauded. Even Dead Bolt clapped.

And it wasn't just that I danced, but I danced dances no one under the age of fifty had ever seen before and with a greased-hipped grace that was inhuman. I had rhythm and I had style and I had all the moves anyone has ever imagined. I had everything but Miranda. She was always on someone else's arm, watching me, her eyebrow raised.

At the end of the night the shoes carried me

outside—I threw the doors wide open in a dramatic move, kicking both my legs out, then flowing into a butt-shaking sidle that carried me to the outside banister, where I slid down and away into the night. But it didn't end there. Under the watchful eye of the full moon, I jitterbugged across streets and through the vacant lot between my street and the school, tap-danced up the steps to the front door, and finally did a grand kick that sent one of the shoes flying off my foot and against the door.

With the thrown shoe, the spell seemed to break. I stopped, breathless.

My legs went rubbery, and I almost collapsed right there from exhaustion. I *hurt*. And not just physically. I slipped off the other shoe and went in in my socks. My mother was already asleep, her snores sawing away at my heartache. She didn't wake to hear my tired footfalls up the stairs to my room.

First thing the next day I called Auntie Kay. "Did they work?" she asked.

"Sure," I said, "they worked great. Great, that is, if I want to dance a bunch of dances that my grandparents danced. If I want to dance *all by myself*." In the corner the shoes sat mute, but I swear that if shoes could smirk, they were smirking.

"Oh, Matt," she said, and then she, like everyone else, laughed.

"It isn't funny!" I shouted. "Old Mrs. Pomeroy told me I was the best jitterbugger she'd ever seen. She tried to dance with me. *Mrs. Pomeroy*. She's at least eighty!"

Auntie Kay just cackled. Finally she got a hold of herself and said, "Mattie, I never said the shoes could dance the new dances. They haven't been used in years, you know."

"So what?"

"So they don't know any dances beyond . . ." I could hear her counting under her breath. When she counted, she counted in Danish, the language she grew up with. "1956 maybe? I don't know when it was that they were last used. I do remember rocking and rolling with—"

" 'Rocking and rolling'? Auntie, you sound like Mom. What am I going to do? I can't go back and do the, the, the—"

"The Lucky Lindy!" she said and burst out laughing again.

"Whatever! I can't do those dances with my friends. I'll look like a freak."

"Then you'll just have to train the shoes in the new dances."

"Oh, great. How am I supposed to do that? I don't *know* the new dances."

"Well, then, little Matt, find someone who does." And she hung up on me.

So I called Miranda.

I know, I know. If I can just call her up, why mess around with the school dances and the shoes? Why not just call her up and ask her to a movie at the mall? Because you can't just call up a girl you like; it isn't done. You need an excuse, preferably a big one. If you, say, ran over her cat with your bike, that would be serious enough to justify a call. Everyone knows this.

"Matt?" she said. "Matt, what do you want?" Her whisper was like a stockinged foot sliding into a slipper.

I gulped. "I was wondering if . . ."

"Yes?" Behind her I could hear the mutter of the television, a kid shouting.

"I thought maybe you might be able to show me how to dance."

She snorted. "Yeah, right. As if you don't know how to dance already. Get real."

"I'm serious," I said. I imagined her showing me how to dance, but no steps you'd ever see at a junior high dance, no, I suddenly pictured myself in her ballerina togs, my arms arched up over my head. *Weird.* I shook my head and said, "Urg."

"I'm serious, too," she said. "If anything, you should be showing *me* how to dance."

"I don't know how to dance," I said, but she snorted again. "Or I don't know the new dances."

"The new dances?" She was listening now.

"Yeah," I said. "The glam slam. The drowning. The zombie drop."

"I know those," she said.

"Really?"

"Did you think I only study ballet?"

"Well, no—I mean, great. You probably know dances I haven't even heard of."

"Like the bounce? The ripper? The runway walk?"

"Yes!" I said.

"Cool." And then there was a long silence. Finally she said, "So why don't you come over this weekend?"

The weirdest thing about Miranda was this: She was just a normal girl. I don't know what I was expecting: maybe that her house would be like a dance studio, that her mom would be a ballerina, that the walls would be mirrored and the floors made of cool wood. Whatever vague ideas I had, they were wrong. Her house was more or less like mine.

We practiced in her cluttered bedroom.

"Sorry about all the Barbies," she said. "I sort of collect them."

"That's cool," I said, and I meant it, though I'd never thought much before of girls who played with Barbies. I pulled the shoes out of my backpack.

"Are you going to wear those?" she asked, pointing.

"They're sort of lucky shoes," I said. "You don't like them?"

"You're such a goof, Matt." She went over to a CD player and was about to press Play when I said, "Let's just do it without music."

"Without music?" She wrinkled her lip.

"I thought it might be easier if we just count time," I said. My aunt had given me this advice earlier that morning. The shoes, Auntie Kay told me, respond to music.

"There was no music after I left the dance," I had said to my aunt.

"Well, that's a good point, but the shoes were probably just . . . enthusiastic."

"Enthusiastic," I repeated.

"Sure. They've been cooped up for forty years, you know. Imagine if you were imprisoned for forty years and then finally released at a dance."

"Yuck."

"In any case, music sets them off. So if you

want to stop dancing, just stop the music. If you need to practice, count time. You know, one-two, one-two-three-four, and so on."

So that afternoon Miranda and I just counted time together. "I don't know why I'm doing this," she said. "This is just so weird." But she wasn't really complaining, and we step-slide-stepped and one-two-one'd the day away. It was wonderful.

But were the shoes paying attention? Did the shoes listen? Did the shoes sit up and take notice? Not at all. Maybe it was the lack of music. Maybe there was no way for them to know which moves went with which songs. Maybe they just like the old dances better.

Whatever the case, the next dance we went to, the shoes did a number on me.

Miranda went as my *date*. Actually, she asked me. I couldn't figure it out.

The minute the band struck up a tune, I found myself hugging Miranda close, turning my cheek against hers, throwing our right arms out straight, and tangoing across the floor. The shoes went so fast I nearly dragged Miranda the last thirty feet.

"I told you I don't know these dances!" she shouted. "Let go!"

"I can't!" I said. It was true, my feet were

not my own. When we reached one end of the floor, I pivoted on my heel, changed position, and tangoed back toward the door.

"Please, Matt!" she pleaded as she stumbled along.

And then one of her feet struck my toe, and I found myself using that gravelly voice again, muttering, "Don't you step on my blue suede shoes!" I twirled her then, rolled her down the length of my arm so that she spun on her feet like a top. She pirouetted away from me and into the crowd. They caught her, and set her on her feet, then everyone applauded. I glimpsed her briefly as she ran weeping from the gym.

But I couldn't go after her, because the shoes had other plans.

We danced the night away, the shoes and I. I stopped trying to look cool after Miranda left, and just screamed as I circled the floor. "Help me!" I shouted out again and again.

"Sure thing, man!" Dead Bolt called back. "You're amazing!" And then he yelled, "Conga line!" and he grabbed on to my hips.

Pretty soon everyone in the gym was lined up behind me, a train of shimmying bodies shadowing my every move. I kicked, they kicked; I threw up my arms and hollered, they did the same. The band dropped all the instruments but the drums, and the drummer gave us a steady rhythm as we circled the floor. We snaked around the gym, in and out of the bathrooms, up and down the grandstands. We duck-walked along the walls, limbo'd under the drinks table, pogo'd under the basketball nets. The drummer kept increasing the pace, and we went faster and faster, kicking and shuffling and wriggling along until a few kids were flung off the back of the line. They screamed going down.

"Slow down!" Dead Bolt called.

But I couldn't. I whipped the line around, and snapped it back upon itself, and listened to the shouts from behind as my classmates were slammed into the walls and each other.

Eventually there were just five of us, hurtling up and down the center of the floor like a runaway train.

"Whoa!" I heard a guy shout, then saw him pinwheel past on the floor.

Dead Bolt let go, and then I was all alone on the dance floor. The whole eighth grade class stood ranked against the wall, silent, while I ran around in ever-tightening circles until, when the rest of the band started up again with a flourish of horns, I dropped to my knees and slid across the floor. I was moving fast, fast enough for my pants to begin to burn under my knees, to smoke; fast enough to cover the length of the gym in four seconds and plow right into the far wall.

When I came to, there was a clutch of faces leaning over me, some of them sipping from punch cups. "Hey," someone said. "He's coming to."

"Muh," I said. My head felt like a popped balloon.

"What'd he say?" It was Dead Bolt.

"Muh," I said again.

"He's calling for his mom!" Everyone laughed.

I shook my head. "Mere—, mere—, mere—"

The heads looked at each other. "Is he saying 'Me'?"

Finally I got it out: "Miranda?"

Dead Bolt dropped a heavy hand onto my shoulder. "Sorry, dude. She split hours ago." Then he brightened and helped me to my feet. "But you were awesome, man! You can really dance!"

Everyone broke into wild applause. I bowed, and kids hooted and hollered and whistled. For the first time in my life I was popular. And I discovered I liked it. I liked it so much that I almost forgot about Miranda.

Almost, but not quite.

*   *   *

I went to her house later that night and threw pebbles at her window. She wouldn't come. Finally I hefted up a rock as big as my fist. It missed the window, but hit the side of the house with a sound like a gunshot.

Lights went on all over the house.

I hid in the bushes until everyone returned to bed, then I went back to the pebbles.

"I knew it was you!" Miranda hissed. "I'll be down in a minute."

She came out in her pajamas underneath a big overcoat. "Let's walk," she said. We did. "Why aren't you wearing your shoes?" she asked after she'd seen me wincing on the gravel drive in my socks.

"Long story," I said. I'd left the shoes next to the bush under her window. No way was I going to wear them.

She nodded and bit her lip and her face crumpled.

Before she could say anything, I said, "Look, I'm really sorry about tonight."

"Are you *trying* to make me look stupid?" she asked. "You make me show you dances and then you dance everything *but* what I showed you."

"It's the shoes," I said.

"Right, Matt," she said, and turned to go

back inside. I ran after her, but my stockinged feet on the gravel slowed me down.

"Miranda!" I called. "Just listen to me, just hear me out."

She turned and sighed and eventually said, "Okay."

I told her everything. She told me that I was the biggest liar she'd ever met. "Even if what you say is true, then you should know I can never dance with you when you're wearing the shoes. I can't keep up." Her head nodded forward. "Listen, it's late, and I've got to get back before my parents discover I'm out here. You should have known better, Matt. What do you need the shoes for? We danced great last weekend. If you can't trust yourself around me, then why should I trust you?"

A good point. Miranda, I thought, should talk to my mother.

Auntie Kay immediately understood what was going on, of course. "You've got a choice," she said. "It's a classic dilemma: popularity and the admiration of your classmates? Or the love of the girl?"

Sheesh. I didn't *love* Miranda, though I must admit she was extraordinarily cool. But I didn't want to be just a dip who couldn't dance again, either.

"So that's it," I said. "The shoes or the girl?"

"These kinds of situations usually end up this way," Auntie Kay said. "There's always a tough decision." She waggled a finger at me. "But remember what I told you: Never choose the shoes over your partner."

And then I realized this "choice" business was bogus. There's no reason I have to have one or the other. Why can't I have both Miranda *and* the shoes in my life? There are two shoes, one left foot and one right foot. But there's nothing in the shoe box that says they have to go on the same pair of feet: The shoes only work together, it's true, but there are two shoes. As Auntie Kay likes to say, it takes two to tango.

And if the dancers hold hands . . .

If you think I wowed the crowds alone, you should see Miranda and me together. We dance old-fashioned dances, but we make them different, we make them our own. Nothing comes out quite right when you wear only one shoe, but then, who remembers how those old dances are supposed to go nowadays? Certainly not our classmates.

"We're making the old dances modern!" Miranda tells me, and she should know. She studies this stuff, after all. When we take our turn

148

on the dance floor, she belts out something about how "we're like another Fred Astaire and Ginger Rogers!"

I just laugh like I know what she's talking about, and I spin her away before I'm tempted to ask, "Another *who?*"

Some people in my family took this story personally. I can't imagine why. . . .

CLEAN AS A WHISTLE

Bruce Coville

Jamie Carhart was, quite possibly, the messiest kid in Minnesota. The messiest kid in her town, no doubt. The county? She pretty well had that sewed up, too. And her mother was convinced that, were there a statewide competition, Jamie would easily be in the top ten, and might, indeed, take first place.

Not that Mrs. Carhart was amused by this fact.

"This room is a sty!" she would say at least once a day, standing in the doorway of Jamie's room and sighing. Then she would poke her foot at the mess that threatened to creep out into the rest of the house, sigh again as if the whole thing was far too much for her to cope with, and wander off.

So it was a shock for Jamie to come home from school on the afternoon of April 17 and find her room totally, perfectly, absolutely neat, clean, and tidy.

"Aaaaaah!" she cried, standing in her doorway. "Aaaaaah! What happened? Who did this?"

Jamie didn't really expect an answer. Her parents both worked and wouldn't be home for another two hours.

For a horrible moment she wondered if her grandmother had come to visit. Gramma Hattie was perfectly capable of sneaking into a kid's room and cleaning it while that kid wasn't looking. Heaven alone knew where *she* might have put things. Even Jamie's mother found Gramma Hattie hard to cope with.

But Gramma Hattie lived in Utah (which in Jamie's opinion was a good place for her), and now that Jamie thought of it, she was off on a trip to Europe. Besides, if she had done this, she would have pounced by now, crowing at her victory over disorder.

So it wasn't her.

Jamie hesitated, wondering if she dared go in.

"Anyone here?" she asked timidly.

No answer.

"Anyone?"

Silence, though she did notice that the cat was on her bed. This did not please her. Actually, she always longed to have the cat in her room. But Mr. Bumpo normally refused to come through her door. Jamie's mother claimed this was because the cat was too neat and couldn't stand the mess. Jamie denied this, usually quite angrily. So she wasn't amused to find Mr. Bumpo here now that the room was so clean; his gently purring presence seemed to confirm her mother's horrible theory.

Jamie looked around nervously as she entered the room. After a moment she dropped her books on her bed. She waited, half expecting someone to come dashing in and pick them up.

"What is going on here?" she asked the cat, scratching its orange-and-black head.

Mr. Bumpo closed his eyes and purred louder.

When Mrs. Carhart arrived home and came up to say hello to Jamie, she grabbed the edges of the doorway and staggered as if she had been hit between the eyes with a two-by-four.

"What," she asked in astonishment, "got into you?"

"What are you talking about?" asked Jamie sourly. She was sitting at her desk, working on a small clay project. She had generated a minor mess with the work, and managed to create a tad of clutter here and there. But overall the room was still so clean as to be unrecognizable.

"I mean this room," said her mother. She squeezed her eyes shut then opened them again, as if to make sure that she wasn't hallucinating. "It's so . . . so . . . *tidy!*"

Jamie looked at her suspiciously. "Didn't you hire someone to come in here and clean it?" she asked. She was still fairly angry about the invasion of her privacy (and not about to admit that she was delighted to find her clay-working tools, which had been missing for some six months now).

Her mother snorted. "The day we can afford a housekeeper, he or she takes on some of *my* work first."

"Then who did this to me?" asked Jamie.

Her mother looked at her oddly. "You are the strangest child," she said at last. "But thanks anyway."

Before Jamie could reply, Mrs. Carhart turned and left. Jamie growled and stabbed a long metal tool through the little clay man she had been making. She knew what her mother was thinking. She was thinking that she, Jamie, had cleaned up the room but was too embarrassed to admit it. She was also thinking that if she pushed the issue Jamie would never do it again. Which meant that when Jamie

claimed she had nothing to do with this . . .
this *catastrophe*, her mother would simply
think that she was playing some weird game,
and the more she tried to convince her other-
wise, the more Mrs. Carhart would be convinced that she was right in her assumption.
Jamie groaned. It was hopeless.

Of course, the other possibility was that her
mother was lying and really had hired someone
to clean the room. Jamie considered the idea.
"Unlikely," she said out loud.

But what other explanation was there? Some
demented prowler who broke into people's
houses to clean rooms when no one was at
home? Jamie glanced around nervously, then
shook her head.

Dinner that night was interesting. Mrs.
Carhart had clearly warned Mr. Carhart that
he was not to make a big deal over the clean
room for fear that Jamie would never do it
again.

By the time the meal was over, Jamie wanted
to scream.

By the time the night was over, she *did*
scream. "I just want you to know that I am *not*
responsible for this!" she bellowed, standing at
the top of the stairs. "I had nothing to do
with it!"

She heard her father chuckle.

Furious, she returned to her room, slamming the door behind her. When she undressed for bed she tore off her clothes and scattered them about the floor. Once she was in her nightgown she went to the door, opened it a crack, and yelled, "Good night!"

Then she slammed it shut and climbed between the sheets.

When Jamie got home the next afternoon, yesterday's clothes (which she had studiously avoided touching that morning) had disappeared from her floor. Her clay-working tools were lined up in an orderly fashion on her desk. The bits of clay that she had left around had been gathered together and rolled into a ball.

The cat was curled up in the middle of her bed, sleeping peacefully.

"Did you do this?" she asked, looking at him suspiciously. She was perfectly aware of what a stupid question it was. On the other hand, when things got this weird, stupid questions began to make sense.

Mr. Bumpo blinked at her, but said nothing. She reached out to stroke him and realized that his fur, which normally had a number of tangles and knots, was perfectly groomed.

"This is creepy," she said. "And I don't like

it." She tossed her backpack on the bed and began to search the room for some clue or sign as to who might have done this. Under her bed she found only that the rapidly breeding colony of dust bunnies had become extinct. She checked her closet next, where she saw something she had not laid eyes on in over three years: the floor. When she looked in her dresser she found that every item of clothing had been neatly folded. This was even worse than it had been the day before!

What she did not find was any sign of who had done this terrible thing to her.

She sat on the edge of her bed for a long time, stroking Mr. Bumpo and listening to him purr. Finally she decided to go back to her clay working. Remembering a sketch for a new project she had made during math class, she overturned her pack and emptied it on the bed. Out tumbled a mixture of books, crumpled papers, pens and pencils in various stages of usefulness, candy wrappers, rubber bands, sparkly rocks she had picked up on the way to and from school, three crayons stuck together with a piece of used chewing gum, and a moldy sandwich.

Jamie dug her way through the mound of stuff until she found the sketch. She carried it to her desk and smoothed it out, then picked up the ball of clay and began to work. After about half an hour she decided to go get a snack.

When she got up from her desk and turned around she let out a yelp of astonishment.

Her bed was perfectly clean! The mess she had dumped onto it had been organized and tidied into meek submission. The crumpled papers had vanished, the pencils were lined up in a tidy row, the crayons unstuck, the gum that held them together mysteriously gone. Even the backpack's straps had been neatly folded beneath it.

"What is going on here?" she cried.

The only answer was a yawn from Mr. Bumpo.

Goose bumps prickling over her arms, Jamie wondered if she should run for her life. But nothing about what was happening was threatening. It was just . . . *weird*.

She stared at her bed for a while, then made a decision. Stomping over to it, she snatched up the neat piles and tossed them into the air. Mr. Bumpo yowled in alarm, bolted from the bed, and ran out of the room. Jamie stirred the mess around a bit more, rumpled the bedcovers for good measure, then went back to her desk and picked up her tools. She pretended to work. What she was really doing was trying to look over her shoulder while bending her neck as little as possible.

For several minutes nothing happened except that her neck got sore. In a way, she was glad nothing happened; part of her had been afraid of what she might see. Eventually the pain in her neck got to be too much, and she was forced to straighten her head. When she turned back she saw a brown blur out of the corner of her eye.

"Gotcha!" she cried, leaping to her feet.

But whatever it was had disappeared.

Jamie stood still for a moment, wondering what had happened. *Under the bed!* she thought suddenly.

Dropping to her knees, she crept to the bed and lifted the edge of the spread. All she saw was clean floor, and a ripple of movement at the other side of the spread. Whatever had been there had escaped.

"That little stinker is fast," Jamie muttered, getting to her feet. She stared at the bed, which was still a mess, and made a decision. Leaving the room, she headed for the kitchen.

When Jamie returned to her room the bed had been remade and the things from her pack were in perfect order. This did not surprise her.

She went to the far side of the bed, the side from which whatever-it-was had disappeared. She opened the bottle of molasses she had

taken from the kitchen, then poured a thick line of the sticky goo the length of the bed, about a foot from the edge. Replacing the lid, she once again messed up everything on top of the bed. Then she returned to her desk.

It wasn't long before she heard a tiny voice cry, "What have you done, what have you done?"

Turning, she saw a manlike creature about a foot-and-a-half tall. He was jumping up and down beside her bed. Covered with brown fur, he looked like a tiny, potbellied version of Bigfoot. The main differences were a long tail and a generally more human face.

"Wretched girl!" cried the creature, shaking a hazelnut-sized fist at her. "What's the matter wi' you?"

"What's the matter with *you*?" she replied. "Sneaking into a person's room and cleaning it up when you're not invited is perverted."

"I was too invited," snapped the creature. Sitting down, he flicked his tail out of the way and began licking molasses from the bottom of his right foot.

"What a liar you are!" said Jamie.

"What a Messy Carruthers you are!" replied the creature. "And you don't know everything, miss. I was sent here by one of your blood. That

counts as invitation if she is close enough—
which she is."

Jamie scowled, then her eyes opened wide.
"My grandmother!" she exclaimed. "*She* sent
you, didn't she?"

"That she did, and I can see why, too. Really,
this place is quite pathetic. I don't understand
why you wouldn't welcome having someone
clean it up. I should think you'd be grateful."

"This is my room, and I liked it the way it
was," said Jamie.

This was not entirely true. Jamie did sometimes wish that the place was clean. But she
felt that she couldn't admit that without los-
ing the argument altogether. Besides, she
mostly did like it her way; and she most certainly did *not* like having someone clean it
without her permission. She felt as if she had
been robbed or something. "What are you, anyway?" she asked, by way of changing the topic.

The creature rolled his eyes, as if he couldn't
believe her stupidity. "I'm a brownie," he said.
"As any fool can plainly see."

"Brownies don't exist."

"Rude!" cried the creature. "Rude, rude,
rude! Your grandmother warned me about that.
'She's a rude girl,' she said. And she was right."

"I think it was rude of my grandmother to

talk about me like that in front of a complete stranger," replied Jamie.

"I'm not a complete stranger. I've been the MacDougal family brownie for nearly three hundred years."

"That shows what you know!" said Jamie. "I'm not a MacDougal, I'm a Carhart."

"Aye, and what was your mother's name before she was married?"

"Chase," said Jamie smugly.

"And her mother's name?"

Jamie's sense of certainty began to fade. "I don't have the slightest idea," she said irritably.

"Rude, and irreverent as well! No sense of family, have you girl? Well I'll tell you what you should have known all along. Your grandmother's maiden name was MacDougal—Harriet Hortense MacDougal, to be precise."

"What has that got to do with me?" asked Jamie.

"Everything," said the brownie. Having finished licking the molasses from his feet, he scooted over to her desk. Moving so fast she barely had time to flinch, he climbed the desk leg and positioned himself in front of her, which made them face-to-face (though his face was barely the size of her fist). "The last of your family in the old country died last year, leaving me without a family to tend to. Your grandmother, bless her heart, came to close up the house. There she found me, moaning and mournful. 'Why, brownie,' she says (she being smart enough to know what I am, unlike some I could mention), 'Why, brownie, whatever is the matter with you?'

" 'My family is all gone,' I told her. 'And now I've naught to care for, so I shall soon fade away.'

"Well, right off your grandmother says, 'Oh, the family is not all gone. I've a daughter in the States, and *she* has a daughter who could more than use your services.' "

"Thanks, Gramma," muttered Jamie.

"I wasn't much interested in coming to this barbarian wilderness," said the brownie, ignoring the interruption. "But things being what they were, I didn't have much choice. So here I am, much to your good fortune."

Jamie wondered for a moment why Gramma Hattie had sent the brownie to her instead of to her mother. It didn't take her long to figure out the answer. Jamie's mother would have been as happy to have someone clean her house as Jamie was annoyed by having her room invaded. Gramma Hattie would never have wanted to do anything that pleasant.

"What will it take to get you to leave me alone?" she asked.

The brownie began to laugh. "What a silly girl you are!" he cried. "You won't ever be alone again!"

Great, thought Jamie, rolling her eyes. *My grandmother has sent me an eighteen-inch-high stalker.* Aloud, she asked, "Are you saying I don't have any choice in this?"

"It's a family matter," replied the brownie. "No one gets to choose when it comes to things like that."

"But I don't want you here!"

The brownie's lower lip began to quiver and his homely little face puckered into what Jamie's mother called "a booper."

"You really don't want me?" he asked, sniffing just a bit.

Jamie felt her annoyance begin to melt, until she realized what the brownie was trying to do to her. (It wasn't hard to figure it out, since she tried the same thing on her parents often enough.) "Oh, stop it," she snapped.

Instantly the brownie's expression changed. Crossing his arms, he sat down on her desk and said, "I'm staying, and that's final."

"You're going, and I mean it," replied Jamie. But she realized even as she said it that she had no way to make the threat stick. The smug look on the brownie's face told her that he was well aware of this.

Now what was she going to do? Totally frustrated, she said, "I'm going to tell my mother about you." She hated talking like that; it made her feel like a little kid. But she couldn't think of anything else.

It didn't make any difference. "She won't believe you," said the brownie, looking even smugger.

"Wouldn't you like to go to work for her?" pleaded Jamie. "She'd be more than happy to have you."

The brownie looked wistful. "I would be delighted," he replied. "But the oldest female in the family has assigned me to you. I have no choice in the matter."

For a day or two Jamie thought she might be able to live with the situation—though with the brownie taking up residence in her closet she made it a point to do her dressing and undressing in the bathroom.

The worst thing was the way her mother smiled whenever she passed the room. Jamie ground her teeth, but said nothing.

By the third day she was getting used to having the room neat and clean. And though she hated to admit it, it was easier to get things done when she didn't have to spend half an hour looking for whatever she needed to start. But just when she was beginning to think that things might work out, the brownie did something unforgivable.

He began to nag.

"Can't you do anything for yourself?" he asked petulantly when she tossed her books on the bed one afternoon after she arrived home from school. "Am I expected to take care of *everything* around here?"

Jamie looked at him in astonishment. "I didn't ask you to come here!" she exploded. "And I certainly didn't ask you to be messing around with my stuff all the time!"

"I am not messing," said the brownie primly. "I am *un*messing."

"I don't care!" she screamed. "I want you to go away. I don't like having you here all the time. I don't like knowing you're in my closet. I don't like having my room look the way you and my grandmother think it should look instead of the way I think it should look."

"Messy Carruthers," muttered the brownie.

"Nosey Parker!" snapped Jamie, accidentally using one of her grandmother's favorite phrases.

She stomped to her desk. The brownie disap-

peared into the closet. A heavy silence descended on the room, broken only when Jamie
crumpled a sketch she didn't like and tossed it
on the floor.

"You pick that up right now!" called the
brownie.

Not only did she not pick up the paper, she
crumpled another and threw it on the floor just
to spite the creature.

That was the beginning of what Jamie later
thought of as "The Great Slob War."

Immediately the brownie came dashing
from the closet, snatched up the offending papers, and tossed them into the wastebasket.
Muttering angrily, he stomped back to the
closet (not very effective for someone only a
foot and a half tall) and slammed the door
behind him.

Jamie immediately wadded up another paper
and threw it on the floor. The brownie dashed
out to pick it up. Seized by inspiration, Jamie
overturned her wastebasket and shook it out.
As the brownie began scurrying around to pick
up the papers, she plunked the wastebasket
down and sat on it. "Now where will you put
the papers?" she asked triumphantly.

Her sense of victory dissolved when the
brownie gathered the trash in a pile and began

to race around it. With a sudden snap, the pile vanished into nothingness. Wiping his hands, the brownie gave her the smuggest look yet. Then he returned to the closet, slamming the door behind him.

"How did you do that?" cried Jamie. He didn't answer. She threw the wastebasket at the door and began to plan her next attack.

She smeared clay on the wall.

She emptied the contents of her dresser onto her floor, tossing out socks, underwear, blouses, and jeans with wild abandon. She tracked all over them with muddy boots and crushed cracker crumbs on top. The brownie simply waited until she left for school. By the time she got home everything had been cleaned, folded, and replaced, neater than before.

Furious, she opened her pencil sharpener and sprinkled its contents all over her bed, topped them off with pancake syrup, a tangled mass of string, and the collection of paper-punch holes she had been saving all year.

The brownie, equally furious, managed to lick and pluck every one of the shavings from the thick weave of the spread with his tiny fingers. The entire time that he was doing this he muttered and cursed, telling Jamie in no uncertain terms what he thought of her, what a disgrace she was to her family, and to what a bad end she was likely to come.

Jamie tipped back her chair on two legs, lounging unrepentantly. "You missed one," she said when the brownie had finished and was heading back to the closet. He raced back to the bed, but after an intense examination discovered that she had been lying.

"What a wicked girl!" he cried. "Trying to fool a poor brownie that way."

"You're not a poor brownie!" she screamed. "You're a menace!" Suddenly days of frustration began to bubble within her. "I can't stand it!" she cried. "I can't take any more of this. I want you to leave me alone!"

"I can't leave you alone!" shouted the brownie, jumping up and down and waving his tiny fists in the air. "We are bound to each other by ancient ties, by words and deeds, by promises written in blood spilled on your family's land."

"Get out!" cried Jamie. In a frenzy she snatched up an old pillow that had come from her grandmother's house and began smacking it against her bed. The pillow burst open, exploding into a cloud of feathers. "Get out, get out, get out!"

Shrieking with rage, the brownie began trying to pick up the feathers. But the faster he moved the more he sent them drifting away from him. When Jamie saw what was happening she began waving her arms to keep the feathers afloat. The brownie leaped and turned, trying to pluck them from the air. He moved faster and faster, wild, frenzied. Finally he began racing in a circle. He went faster still, until he was little more than a blur to Jamie's eyes. Then, with a sudden *snap!* he vanished, just as the papers had the day before.

Jamie blinked, then began to laugh. She had done it. She had gotten rid of him!

And that should have been that.

But a strange thing happened. As the days went on she began to miss the little creature. Infuriating as he had been, he had also been rather cute. Moreover, the condition of her room began to irritate her.

A week after the brownie vanished she was rooting around in the disarray of her floor, trying to find her clay-working tools, which had been missing for three days. Forty-five minutes of searching had so far failed to turn them up.

"Sometimes I actually wish that brownie had stayed around," she muttered.

From the closet a tiny voice said, "A-hoo."

Jamie stood up. "Is that you, brownie?"

"A-hoo," repeated the voice; it sounded pathetically weak.

Feeling slightly nervous—ever since this started she had not been entirely comfortable with her closet—Jamie went to the door and asked, "Are you in there?"

"A-hoo," said the voice a third time. It seemed to come from the upper shelf.

"Brownie, is that you?"

No answer at all this time.

She ran to her desk. Kicking aside the intervening clutter, she dragged the chair back to the closet. By standing on it, she could reach the upper shelf.

"Brownie?" she called. "Are you there?"

"A-hoo."

The voice was coming from an old cardboard box. She pulled it from the shelf and looked in. The brownie lay inside. He looked wan and thin, and after a moment she realized to her horror that she could see right through him.

"I thought you had left," she said, her voice thick with guilt.

"I had no place to go." His voice seemed to come from a far-off place. "I am bound to you, and to this house. All I could do was wait to fade away."

An icy fear clenched her heart. "Are you going to die?"

"A-hoo," said the brownie. Then he closed his eyes and turned his head away.

She scrambled from the chair and placed the shoe box on her bed. *I've killed him!* she thought in horror. Reaching into the box, she lifted his tiny form. It was no heavier than the feathers he had been chasing when he had disappeared. She could see her fingers right through his body.

"Don't die," she pleaded. "Don't. Stay with me, brownie. We can work something out."

The brownie's eyelids fluttered.

"I mean it!" said Jamie. "I was actually starting to miss you."

"A-hoo," said the brownie. Opening his eyes, he gazed at her uncomprehendingly. "Oh, it's you," he said at last. Then he lifted his head and looked at her room. He moaned tragically at the disarray and closed his eyes again.

"I'll clean it up," she said hastily. "Just don't die. Promise?"

The brownie coughed and seemed to flicker, as if he was going to vanish altogether. "A-hoo," he said again.

"Watch!" said Jamie. Placing him gently on the bed, she began a whirlwind cleaning campaign, moving almost as fast as the brownie himself when he was in a cleaning frenzy. Along the way she found her clay-working tools, the pendant her nice grandmother had sent her, two dollars and forty-seven cents in change, and the missing homework that had cost her an F the day before. She kept glancing at the brownie while she worked and was encouraged to see that he seemed to be getting a little more solid. When she was entirely done she turned around and said, "There! See?"

To her enormous annoyance, the brownie had turned the box over and was sitting on the end of it, looking as solid as a brick and smiling broadly. "Well done!" he said.

"I thought you were dying!" she said angrily.

"I wasn't dying, I was fading. And if you wanted me to live, why are you so angry that I'm alive?"

"Because you were faking!" she snarled.

"I never!" cried the brownie, sounding genuinely offended. "Another few minutes and I would have been gone for good, faded away like a summer breeze, like the last coals in the fire, like dew in the morning sun, like—"

"All right, all right," said Jamie. "I get the picture." She paused. Though she still wasn't sure she believed him, she asked, "What happens when you fade?"

The brownie shivered, and the look of terror on his face was so convincing that she began to suspect that he was telling the truth. "I'm just *gone*," he said.

Jamie shivered, too. "Do you really have nowhere else to go?" she asked.

The brownie shook his head. " 'Tis you to whom I'm bound, and you with whom I must stay until the day I fade away—or the day you become the oldest female in the family and assign me to someone else of your line."

Jamie sighed. She looked at the pendant, the tools, the change lying on her desk. "If I let you stay will you behave?"

The brownie wrapped his tail around his knees. "I am what I am," he said.

"So am I," she replied.

The brownie looked startled, as if this had not occurred to him before. "Can you help a little?" he asked plaintively.

"If I do, will you stop nagging me?"

The brownie considered this for a moment. "Will you let me keep the closet as neat as I want?"

"Can I have my desk as messy as I want?" replied Jamie.

The brownie glanced at the desk, shivered, then nodded.

"It's a deal," said Jamie.

And so it was. They did not, it should be noted, exactly live happily ever after. The truth is, they annoyed each other a great deal over the years. However, they also learned to laugh together, and had enormous good times when they weren't fighting.

That's the way it goes with family things.

ABOUT THE AUTHORS

STEPHEN GOLDIN is the author of numerous short stories and more than twenty-five science fiction and fantasy books, including *The Eternity Brigade* and the Parsina Saga, and has collaborated with wife Mary Mason on the "Jade Darcy" series. He also helped design the computer game *Star Trek: The Next Generation: "A Final Unity."* He lives in Alameda, California.

NINA KIRIKI HOFFMAN grew up in Southern California and had many peculiar neighbors, some of whom inspired her stories about the LaZelle family. Her stories have appeared in magazines and in anthologies like *A Nightmare's Dozen* and several in this series. Her *Body Switchers from Outer Space* is part of *R.L. Stine's Ghosts of Fear Street* series, and she has published two other novels. She lives in Oregon.

LAWRENCE SCHIMEL has published stories and poems in over a hundred anthologies—including some in this series, as well as *School Supplies* and *Weird Tales from Shakespeare*—and in many magazines, including *Cricket* and *Spider*. He has also edited several anthologies himself, such as *Tarot Fantastic* and *Yankee Vampires*. He lives in New York City.

DEBORAH WHEELER has been a bacteriologist, a librarian, and a preschool gym teacher. In between two children, a black belt in kung fu san soo, and a chiropractic career, she's published two novels—*Jaydium* and *Northlight*—and three dozen short stories. She lives in Los Angeles.

TERRY JONES was a member of the Monty Python comedy group and directed their film *Monty Python's Life of Brian*. He attended Oxford University and has a special interest in medieval history and literature. "The Wooden City" is from a collection of fairy tales he originally wrote for his daughter.

PATRICIA C. WREDE was born in Chicago and started writing in seventh grade. Today she has published over a dozen books, including *Shadow Magic* and *Talking to Dragons*, and is part of the Liavek shared-world anthology. She lives in Minneapolis with her three cats.

About the Authors

ALICE DeLaCROIX is the author of *Mattie's Whisper*, a middle-grade novel, and has contributed to *Highlights* magazine. She lives in the country with her husband, two children, three horses, a dog and cat, and many trees.

MARGARET BECHARD is the author of several books for young readers, including *Star Hatchling*, a science fiction novel. She lives in Tigard, Oregon, with her husband and their three sons. They have one cat, but no unicorns. Yet.

JOHN GREGORY BETANCOURT has written eleven science fiction and fantasy novels, including two best-selling *Star Trek* books. He also runs a publishing company, Wildside Press, with his wife, and writes novels based on films and television shows like *Lois & Clark: The New Adventures of Superman*.

MICHAEL STEARNS can't dance, but that hasn't stopped him from editing the young adult anthologies *A Wizard's Dozen*, *A Starfarer's Dozen*, and *A Nightmare's Dozen*. His story "Gone to Pieces" appeared in *Bruce Coville's Book of Nightmares II*. He lives in San Diego with his cat.

About the Authors

JOHN PIERARD has illustrated all the books in this series, as well as the *My Teacher Is an Alien* quartet, the popular *My Babysitter Is a Vampire* series, and stories in *Isaac Asimov's Science Fiction Magazine*. He lives in New York City.

Photo: Jules

BRUCE COVILLE was born and raised in a rural area of central New York. He spent his early years dodging cows and chores, and dreaming about finding real magic. He first fell under the spell of writing when his sixth-grade teacher (a true miracle worker) gave the class an extended period of time to work on a short story.

Sixteen years later—after stints as a toymaker, a gravedigger, and an elementary school teacher—Bruce published *The Foolish Giant*, a picture book illustrated by his wife and frequent collaborator, Katherine Coville. Since then Bruce has published nearly sixty books for young readers. Many of them, such as *Into the Land of the Unicorns, Goblins in the Castle,* and *The World's Worst Fairy Godmother,* are filled with magical events.

These days Bruce and Katherine live in an old brick house in Syracuse with their youngest child, Adam; their Norwegian elkhound, Thor; and three cats, including an enchanted kitty named Princess Ozma Fuzzybutt.